D1261192

Virginia Woolf

Virginia Woolf

An Annotated Bibliography of Criticism
1915-1974

Robin Majumdar

Garland Publishing, Inc., New York & London

1976

Copyright © 1976

by Robin Majumdar

All Rights Reserved

Library of Congress Cataloging in Publication Data

Majumdar, Robin.
   Virginia Woolf : an annotated bibliography of
criticism, 1915-1974.

   (Garland reference library of the humanities ;
v. 42)
   Bibliography: p.
   Includes index.
   1. Woolf, Virginia Stephen, 1882-1941--Bibliog-
raphy.
Z8984.2.M33 [PR6045.072]   016.823'9'12
ISBN 0-8240-9961-3   75-24893

Printed in the United States of America

For My Mother

CONTENTS

PREFACE

Virginia Woolf's books have received serious critical attention
not only in Britain and America but also in many other countries.
There is, therefore, a need for a complete bibliography repre-
senting the varying critical attitudes to Mrs. Woolf's work. The
present book is an attempt in that direction. B. J. Kirkpatrick's
excellent bibliography of Virginia Woolf provides a chronolgoical
account of Mrs. Woolf's own writings. Dr. Kirkpatrick does not
include the criticism of Virginia Woolf's works, because it is
not within the scope of her book. Maurice Beebe's checklist in
MODERN FICTION STUDIES (February 1956) is 'selected' and
leaves out of account some important items. I have listed almost
all the items published between 1915 and 1974 and annotated most
of them. It has not, however, been possible for me to annotate
some articles and books on Virginia Woolf in English and foreign
languages which were not available to me. In the Introduction I
have discussed the various trends in Virginia Woolf criticism
and the development of her critical reputation.

This work is mainly based on the bibliography of my thesis on
Virginia Woolf for which the University of London awarded me a
doctorate. I am greatly indebted to Dr. Charles Peake, my super-
visor at London University, whose encouragement and assistance
have been invaluable. I am also grateful to my friend, Mr. Peter

ix

Dixon, Reader in English, Westfield College, London, for his
helpful suggestions. Thanks are also due to my students, Mr.
Narendra Ghosh and Miss Lopa Chatterjee for help at various
levels.

Presidency College,
Calcutta,

October   1975   R. M.

x

INTRODUCTION

"My position is ambiguous. I'm fundamentally, I think, an out-
sider," Virginia Woolf once said,[1] and so indeed she was. Her
books evoked various responses, ranging from adulation to denigra-
tion. There was no critical consensus concerning her work, as
there could hardly be, when her unconventional art evoked such a
variety of reactions. Her work received serious critical attention not only in Britain and America but also in many other
countries. Her novels alone received no fewer than 340 reviews
and more than forty articles dealt specifically with her fiction.
Besides, numerous books and articles touched on various aspects
of her work.

A number of influences were instrumental in shaping Virginia
Woolf's critical reputation. The changing trends in Woolf criticism were influenced by the contemporary climate of critical
opinion as well as by the socio-political situation of the time.
Sometimes, as in the thirties, besides purely literary criteria,
extrinsic factors such as the Marxist ideology influenced critical
response to Mrs. Woolf's novels. Hardly less influential was the
emergence of SCRUTINY as an arbiter of critical taste. F. R.
Leavis's critical criteria had a powerful impact on an important
section of contemporary opinion about Virginia Woolf's work.

---

1.   See A WRITER'S DIARY, ed. Leonard Woolf, Lond., 1965, p. 308.

Although ORLANDO and THE YEARS were popular books, the reading
public had, in general, no great taste for her novels. The public demand was for the kind of fiction which had familiar characters and absorbing action. The common complaint against her
was that she was difficult, she was obscure. This was the reason
why the general public preferred her non-fiction to her fiction.
The clarity, lucidity, wit and humour of her non-fictional writings pleased those readers who were bored with her stream of
consciousness method. The fact of the case was that Virginia
Woolf's subtle techniques demanded the kind of mental effort
of which the ordinary reader was not capable. She did not ex-
ploit the stock responses of the common reader nor did she use
the clichés of the popular novel.

The quality of contemporary criticism was very uneven. There was
often much vague talk of Virginia Woolf's form and characterization but little awareness of her intentions. Many critics merely
echoed the popular views and showed little insight into the
mechanics of Mrs. Woolf's new craft.

The controversy over Virginia Woolf's fiction centred, in the
main, on her theory of the novel. The central problem which
engaged most critical attention was about her conception of the
novel in terms of poetry. The point at issue was whether a subjective, lyrical approach to fiction such as Virginia Woolf's

was appropriate to the novel as an art-form, whether the traditional rationale of fiction could altogether be rejected. In
general, Virginia Woolf's subjective technique, her use of the
novel as a vehicle for sensitive, lyrical moods received more
blame than praise /Nos. 106; 273; 389; 397; 515/. Most critics
maintained that Mrs. Woolf was writing not novels but poetry in
prose. This opinion proceeded from the assumption that there
was no place for poetry in the novel which had its own conven-
tions. The poetry-novel dichotomy dominated much Woolf criticism
in the twenties and thirties /Nos. 157; 397/. The articles
/No. 397/ by the American critic William Troy are obviously
based on this postulate. Mrs. Woolf's poetic style was also
viewed critically by several other critics, Empson /No. 151/
and Peel /No. 321/ in particular.

According to many critics, it is Virginia Woolf's poetic method
which is responsible for the 'unsatisfactory' characterization
and construction of her novels. They objected to her presentation of human beings from the inside. Her characters seemed
to them vague and shadow-like spirits rather than robust and
solid /Nos. 118; 120; 156; 269; 301; 304/. It was only her
characters in TO THE LIGHTHOUSE who received some approval,
because the critics found them more tangible than her previous
portraits. Even such a hostile critic of Virginia Woolf as
Arnold Bennett said that there was an 'improvement' in her

character-drawing in this novel   /̄See No. 773̄/.

Mrs. Woolf's novels were also condemned for what seeemed to most
critics their fragmentary structure. They complained that what
she did was simply to present a series of fleeting impressions
which she did not bother to integrate. Consequently, the framework of her fiction was shapeless and amorphous. As for plots
and incidents, there was little in her novels and everything was
subordinated to her preoccupation with consciousness   /̄Nos.
105-6; 151; 258; 361̄/.

It is interesting to note that the critical attitudes to Virginia
Woolf's character-presentation in her first two novels were not
quite as harsh as those to her later portraits   /̄Nos. 656-7;
691̄/. The reason was simple. In these early works Mrs. Woolf
had not yet turned her back on the traditional novelist's objective conception of character as she did in her later mature
novels. Similarly, as these novels were not entirely untradi-
tional in their form, their structure was not so severely criticized as was that of the later experimental novels. NIGHT AND
DAY, for instance, received high praise for its meticulous and
well-knit construction   /̄No. 690̄/. And the chief reason why
among the later novels ORLANDO and TO THE LIGHTHOUSE were more
popular was that they were less introspective and followed a more
or less continuous narrative pattern. But how far were these

criticisms of Woolf's novels valid? Surely, the critics judged
Virginia Woolf by the traditional categories of the novel. But
were these criteria absolutes? Were they relevant to the kind
of fiction Mrs. Woolf wrote? These questions were worth ask-
ing and several critics did ask them /Nos. 7; 10; 14; 18; 25;
52; 88; 111/. They attempted to relate Virginia Woolf's work
to her individual perspective. Of course, they evaluated her
intentions and did not always approve of them. This was, to
be sure, the beginning of a new approach to Woolf's fiction. At
a time when criticism was dominated by certain preconceptions
this new attitude was necessary for the understanding and appreciation of Virginia Woolf's novels. Clive Bell /No. 88/, for
instance, provided a new insight into the question of Mrs. Woolf's
style. Bell's analysis, refreshingly free from prepossessions,
was a laudable attempt to examine Woolf's work on her own terms.
E. M. Forster's articles /Nos. 156-57/ were also valuable contri-
butions to this critical approach. Forster considered Virginia
Woolf's characterization as a weakness, but he was quick to
seize on her specific gift: her power to convey the 'actual
process of thinking'. Similar discrimination characterized
several other contemporary studies. Although routine complaints
about Mrs. Woolf's novels--their insubstantial characterization
and fluid construction,etc.--continued, a new critical sophisti-

cation was increasingly evident, an effort was being made to investigate the real nature of Mrs. Woolf's sensibility and the character of her equipment. The close relation between Virginia Woolf's view of life and her fiction was stressed by the critics who adopted this line of approach. They attempted to explain the characterization and the form of Mrs. Woolf's novels in terms of her particular conception of life as a flux /̅Nos. 7; 18; 43/̅. In this respect some of the post-war studies of Woolf's fiction, especially those by Joan Bennett /̅No. 7 /̅, Jean Guiguet /̅No. 25/̅, James Hafley /̅No 26/̅ and David Daiches /̅No. 18/̅ stand out for their discrimination and understanding.

One major issue in Woolf criticism was her subjective view of reality. Her conception of reality as an inner spiritual experience, a 'luminous halo', was often the target of attack in critical circles. The usual charge against her was that she dealt with a very limited area of human experience and that her contacts with the objective and temporal world were insignificant. Her excessive refinement and sophistication and aloofness from the 'raw stuff of life' provoked hostile reactions /̅See Nos. 65; 81; 208; 295; 397/̅. J. F. Holms's review-article /̅No. 223/̅ foreshadowed this trend in Woolf criticism. Holms saw in the thoughts, emotions and motives of the characters in MRS. DALLOWAY pure sentimentality, bearing little 'relation to the truth of life'. Evidently, he did not find the characters 'real' because they did not conform to his view of the objective and temporal reality of fictional characters. The criticisms of Conrad Aiken /No. 65_7 and W. L. George /No. 55_7_7, though less harsh, were along similar lines.

In the thirties the anti-aesthetic reaction against Virginia Woolf's work gathered further momentum. It received a powerful impetus from the contemporary socio-political scene on the one hand, and from the impact of the Marxian ideology on the other. The Marxist case against Woolf was that she did not deal with the 'real' world /See Nos. 130; 528; 60_1_7. Undoubtedly, by the real world the Marxist critics meant economic and social realities rather than mental phenomena. Interestingly, a few critics who also discussed Woolf's work from the sociological standpoint reached conclusions which were very different from those of the Marxists. Instead of condemning Virginia Woolf as a bourgeois writer with no social consciousness, they maintained that Mrs. Woolf was deeply influenced by the socio-political forces of her time. Such issues as women's liberation and class distinction did affect her. This viewpoint emerged clearly in the discussions of Margaret Blanchard /No. 97_7 among others.

In another direction, F. R. Leavis and his followers attacked Virginia Woolf for what they called her 'obsession' with purely aesthetic sensibility and her lack of concern with moral issues.

They were particularly critical of her preoccupation with the 'fine' shades of consciousness and her detachment from the world outside. Leavis's review-article /No. 258/ was a typical example of this line of attack which was also evident in the appraisals of Bradbrook /No. 106/, Mellers /No. 286/, Savage /No. 361/, Rahv /No. 330/ and a few others /See Nos. 567; 578/. But it was not only the Marxist and the SCRUTINY critics who criticized Virginia Woolf's 'aloofness' and 'over-refinement' but many others also did so.

It would be unfair to deny the value of these sociological and moral approaches. Their excesses apart, these critics helped to point out the dangers of a too aesthetic approach to literature. But they could not fully invalidate the argument that Mrs. Woolf's novels were real and showed concern with moral values, although she had different ideas of the nature of reality and the nature of morality. This viewpoint was put forward by several critics in post-war years. Against the diatribe of the Marxists and the Leavisites these critics attempted to defend Virginia Woolf from the charge of aesthetic dilettantism. They thought that Mrs. Woolf was very much aware of the nature of the contemporary human predicament and that in her preoccupation with the loneliness of the individual and the passionate longing for the integration of the human personality, Mrs. Woolf dealt with a major problem of modern life. They argued that because of the social and cultural

xviii

disintegration the inner mental experiences of the individual were for Virginia Woolf the only reality. Her constant endeavour was to search for a synthesis, a harmony in the confused and bewildered life of the post-war man /See Nos. 7; 14; 25;42; 83; 104/. This sort of revaluation was a big advance in Woolf criticism.

A close analysis of the text was a remarkable feature of some Woolf criticism. Critical attention centered on the minute scrutiny of the novels' texture--the words, symbols, images and the technical devices employed. Daiches's analysis of the interior monologue in MRS. DALLOWAY provides a brilliant example of this kind of method /No. 137/. Empson's study of TO THE LIGHTHOUSE illustrates much the same kind of procedure /See No. 151/. Close exegeses have also revealed various layers of meaning, especially in TO THE LIGHTHOUSE. Irene Simon's detailed examination /See No. 374/ of the use and significance of the imagery in Woolf's major novels was a solid contribution to the structural criticism of her fiction. Several recent appraisals of Virginia Woolf have been concerned with some specific problems and aspects of her novels /See Nos. 100; 129; 159/. Serious attention has also been paid to the analysis of the stylistic and linguistic peculiarities of Mrs. Woolf's novels.

Extra-literary factors such as group spirit and prejudice played

xix

no small part in the development of Virginia Woolf's reputation.
Not a few critics were prejudiced by their repugnance towards
Bloomsbury. In several cases attacks on her work were, in the
ultimate analysis, attacks on the Bloomsbury Group as a whole.
A strong anti-Bloomsbury bias influenced--and prejudiced--some
critics' judgements about her work /See Nos. 221; 258; 389/.

Bloomsbury was to many critics the home of intellectual snobbery
and aesthetic dilettantism cut off from the common earth. But
the anti-Bloomsbury spirit did not bias all the verdicts on Woolf.
Free from preconceptions and reservations, several critics attempted to show the importance of the Bloomsbury philosophy for
a clear understanding of Mrs. Woolf's aesthetics and her values.
Among others, Irma Rantavaara /No. 50/ and Jean Guiguet /No. 25/
considered her work against the Bloomsbury milieu.

Virginia Woolf's feminist pieces aroused various reactions. Some
regarded them as mere propaganda and criticized her 'partisan'
and 'militant' attitude /See Nos. 1038; 1040/. But a few others
/Nos. 39; 79; 80; 236/ thought that what Virginia Woolf was plead-
ing for in A ROOM OF ONE'S OWN and THREE GUINEAS was not any
hostility between the sexes but the androgynous human personality.
Her motto was the marriage of opposites, the combination of
masculine intellect and feminine intuition. The conception of
androgyny   was, according to these critics, basic

to Mrs. Woolf's feminist doctrine.

Virginia Woolf's relationship with other writers and thinkers
was the subject of several discussions of her work /See Nos.
242; 376/. Dostoevsky's influence on Woolf was closely examined
/See Nos. 308; 315; 350/ and so was the affinity between Virginia
Woolf's view of fiction and that of the Russian novelists /No.
323/. The impact of Freudian psychology and the Bergsonian
durée on Woolf's fiction interested several scholars /Nos. 129;
143; 222/.

Virginia Woolf's reputation among the continental critics was
generally high. In France she was greatly esteemed. Such famous
French critics as André Maurois and Jacques-Emile Blanche admired
her work. Maurois praised her psychological insight and lyrical
prose /Nos. 277; 595/. Several other critics also wrote sen-
sitively on her art. Floris Delattre /No. 142/ and J. J. Mayox
/No. 279/ dealt with such important aspects of Woolf's novels as
the space-time relations and the Bergsonian durée. A few critics
in France had, however, some reservations about Virginia Woolf's
experiments in fiction. Paul Dottin /No. 149/, for instance,
praised her language and symbolism but disliked her 'indirect
style', and Gabriel Marcel /No. 273/ also disapproved of her
method in THE WAVES.

In Italy too Virginia Woolf's novels received serious attention, though it was much less than that in France. Salavator Rosati's article /No. 345/ was one of the best commentaries on Woolf's technique in ORLANDO and his interpretation of the book's symbolism showed critical acumen of a high order.

In Germany Woolf's work evoked no small interest. One of the earliest critical studies of her novels was by a critic from Germany, Ruth Gruber /No. 24/. And of the several contemporary essays on Virginia Woolf in Germany the one by Walter Neuschäffer /No. 308/ is particularly good. He was among those critics who discussed the very relevant and interesting question of Woolf's affinity in theme and technique with the Russian novelists.

But Virginia Woolf's reputation was not limited to Europe and to the United States. She was well-known in other countries too. Even in Asia and South America /60; 366/ her work aroused no small critical interest. It will be seen from the bibliography that in both India and Japan Woolf's novels excited serious critical attention /See Nos. 123; 239; 245-49; 272; 355-6/.

I.   BOOKS ON VIRGINIA WOOLF

1   Alexander, Jean.   THE VENTURE OF FORM IN THE NOVELS OF VIRGINIA
    WOOLF. New York, 1974.

2   Amoruso, Vito.   VIRGINIA WOOLF.   Bari: Adriatica Editrice,
    1968 (in Italian).

3   Badenhausen, O.   DIE SPRACHE VIRGINIA WOOLFS.   Marburg, 1932.

4   Bazin, Nancy T.   VIRGINIA WOOLF AND THE ANDROGYNOUS VISION.
    New Brunswick, New Jersey, 1973.

5   Beja, Morris (ed.).   VIRGINIA WOOLF: TO THE LIGHTHOUSE.   A
    Case Book. Lond., 1970.

6   Bell, Quentin.   VIRGINIA WOOLF: A BIOGRAPHY.   Vols. I and II,
    Lond., 1972.

    Discusses the chief facts of Virginia Woolf's life: her mental
    illness, marriage, sensitivity to the reception of her books,
    'snobbery' and 'arrogance', etc. A balanced biography 'encom-
    passing detachment and involvement.'

    REVIEWED:

    (a)   THE GUARDIAN.   Lond., June 14, 1972, p. 9.
    (b)   Holroyd, Michael.   THE TIMES.   Lond., June 15, 1972, p. 7.
    (c)   Pritchett, V. S.   THE NEW STATESMAN.   Lond., June 1972,
          pp. 827-8.
    (d)   Spender, Stephen.   THE SPECTATOR.   Lond., June 1972, 936-
          7.
    (e)   Spender, Stephen.   LONDON MAGAZINE.   Vol. 12, No. 6,
          March 1973, 137-140.
    (f)   Oberbeck, S. K.   NEWSWEEK. New York, 126, 80,   November 20,
          1972.
    (g)   Weintraub, S.   NEW REPUBLIC. New York, 167:   33, November
          25, 1972.
    (h)   De Matt.   SATURDAY REVIEW.   New York, 55, December 9,
          1972.
    (i)   Duffy, Martha.   TIME.   Chicago, November 20, 1972, 49-50.

7   Bennett, Joan.   VIRGINIA WOOLF: HER ART AS A NOVELIST.   Cam-
    bridge, 1945.

    A penetrating discussion of Virginia Woolf's novels in relation
    to her vision of life. Argues persuasively that Mrs. Woolf's
    characterization and construction are unlike those of the tradi-
    tional novel, because her purpose as a novelist was to empha-
    size the fluidity and flux of modern life. The author stresses
    the need to understand Woolf's individual perspective.

REVIEWED:

(a) THE TIMES LITERARY SUPPLEMENT. LOND., July 21, 1945, p. 344.
(b) THE CAMBRIDGE REVIEW. Cambridge, May 26, 1945, p. 355.
(c) Tomkins, J. M. S. THE REVIEW OF ENGLISH STUDIES. Lond., October 1945, p. 337.
(d) White, Beatrice. THE MODERN LANGUAGE REVIEW. Washington, January 1946, 78-79.
(e) S. C. C. THE CHRISTIAN SCIENCE MONITOR. Boston, October 13, 1945, p. 20.
(f) Linn, Bettina. THE YALE REVIEW. New Haven, December 1945, 360-61.
(g) Lehmann, Rosamond. NEW STATESMAN AND NATION. Lond., March 3, 1945, p. 143.
(h) Peschmann, Herman. THE WIND AND THE RAIN. Lond., Summer 1945, 45-48.
(i) Koch, Vivienne. THE SEWANEE REVIEW. Autumn 1946, 727-731.
(j) Spencer, Theodore. THE NEW REPUBLIC. New York, December 3, 1945, 758-760.
(k) Allen, Walter. TIME AND TIDE. Lond., March 17, 1945, 220-230.
(l) H. P. E. PUNCH. Lond., February 11, 1945, p. 169.

8 Bizé, Paul. VIRGINIA WOOLF AS A LITERARY ARTIST (Mémoire Présenté à la Faculté des Lettres de Lille,Pour le diplome d'Etudes Superieures d'anglais) Paris, July 1930.

9 Blackstone, Bernard. VIRGINIA WOOLF: A COMMENTARY. Lond., 1949.

The approach is philosophical. Sees Virginia Woolf as a mystic and as a seer. Suggests that Woolf was a metaphysical writer who broke away from the conventional craft of fiction because she needed a different kind of pattern for her philosophical perspective. The special value of the study lies in its perceptive enquiry into the nature of Virginia Woolf's genius.

REVIEWED:

(a) Lehmann, John. TIME AND TIDE. Lond., April 9, 1949.
(b) Willy, Margaret. ENGLISH. Lond., Vol. 7, No. 42, Autumn 1949, p. 297.
(c) Smith, Steve. THE SPECTATOR. Lond., March 25, 1949, p. 405.
(d) Crosbie, Mary. JOHN O'LONDON'S WEEKLY. Lond., May 13, 1949, p. 293.
(e) Redman, Ben Ray. THE SATURDAY REVIEW OF LITERATURE. New York, July 23, 1949, p. 18.
(f) Frisbie, George. THE NEW YORK HERALD TRIBUNE. September 4, 1949, p. 5.

(g)   THE TIMES LITERARY SUPPLEMENT. Lond., April 23, 1949,
      p. 266.

10   Blackstone, Bernard. VIRGINIA WOOLF (Writers and Their Work).
     Lond., 1952.

     Much the same line of approach as in his earlier book.
     Virginia Woolf's novels centre on a common theme: man's
     search for the inner life, for the still centre.

11   Brandt, Magdalene. REALISMUS UND REALITAT IM MODERNEN ROMAN:
     METHODOLOGISCHE UNTERSUCHUNGEN ZU VIRGINIA WOOLFS THE WAVES.
     Bad Homburg: Gehlen, 1968.

12   Brewster, Dorothy. VIRGINIA WOOLF'S LONDON. Lond., 1959.

     Discusses the importance of London as a background and a set-
     ting in Virginia Woof's novels. Refers to THE YEARS as a
     typical example.

     REVIEWED:

     (a)   Berman, Ronald. SEWANEE REVIEW. LXXII, I, Wint. 1964,
           163-64.
     (b)   Dunn, Esther. NEW YORK HERALD TRIBUNE. April 24, 1960,
           p. 4.
     (c)   THE TIMES LITERARY SUPPLEMENT. January 15, 1960, p. 35.
     (d)   NEW YORK TIMES. May 8, 1960, p. 7.
     (e)   THE SATURDAY REVIEW. New York, May 21, 1960, 54-55.

13   Brewster, Dorothy. VIRGINIA WOOLF. Lond., 1963.

     Gives plot summaries of Virginia Woolf's novels. More factual
     than critical. Little discussion or evaluation of Woolf's
     work. The chapter on Virginia Woolf's interest in Russian
     fiction is interesting. Contains valuable quotations from
     the unpublished correspondence between Virginia Woolf and her
     friend Charles Percy Sanger.

     REVIEWED:

     (a)   Brophy, Brigid. THE NEW STATESMAN AND NATION. March
           29, 1963, 463-64.
     (b)   Beer, J. B. THE REVIEW OF ENGLISH STUDIES. May 1964,
           p. 219.
     (c)   THE TIMES LITERARY SUPPLEMENT. Lond., March 22, 1963,
           p. 202.
     (d)   Lehmann, John. THE LISTENER. April 4, 1963, p. 605.

14   Chambers, R. L. THE NOVELS OF VIRGINIA WOOLF. Edinburgh, 1947.

A judicious assessment of Woolf's contemporary significance. Takes issue with those who describe Mrs. Woolf as a mere aesthete. Asserts that Mrs. Woolf concerned herself with the central problem of her generation: the individual's essential loneliness. Analyses the development of Virginia Woolf's technique. Particularly good on the three middle novels.

REVIEWED:

(a) Pritchett, V. S. THE NEW STATESMAN AND NATION. December 27, 1947, p. 511.
(b) MacCarthy, Desmond. THE SUNDAY TIMES. Lond., December 28, 1947, p. 3.
(c) Savage, D. S. THE SPECTATOR. Lond., 1947, p. 3.
(d) THE TIMES LITERARY SUPPLEMENT. Lond., February 7, 1948, p. 80.

15   Chastaing, M. LA PHILOSOPHIE DE VIRGINIA WOOLF. Paris, 1951.

16   Clare, M. E. ALGO SOBRE VIRGINIA WOOLF. Santiago, Chile, 1967.

17   Collins, Robert G. VIRGINIA WOOLF'S BLACK ARROWS OF SENSATION: THE WAVES (The Modern Novelist and The Modern Novel). Ilfracombe, 1962.

18   Daiches, David. VIRGINIA WOOLF (New Directions). Connecticut, U.S.A.,1942, Lond., 1945.

A more balanced judgement of Virginia Woolf's work than the usual verdicts on her. Daiches evaluates Mrs. Woolf's work in terms of her perspective although he has reservations about her method and finds her world a little too refined. Discusses, inter alia, the experimental nature of Virginia Woolf's technique, and its relation to the contemporary background. Provides an extremely able analysis of the interior monologue in MRS. DALLOWAY.

REVIEWED:

(a) Garnett, David. THE NEW STATESMAN AND NATION. September 22, 1945, 198-199.
(b) R. M. F. THE DUBLIN MAGAZINE. October-December, 1945, p. 63.
(c) Scott, Winfield. THE AMERICAN MERCURY. New York, November 1942, 628-30.
(d) THE LISTENER. Lond., July 5, 1945, p. 21.
(e) Bosanquet, Theodore. TIME AND TIDE. Lond., July 21, 1945, p. 607.

19   Davenport, W. A. TO THE LIGHTHOUSE (Notes on English Liter-
      ature). Oxford, 1969.

      Discusses with reference to TO THE LIGHTHOUSE the general
      characteristics of Virginia Woolf's art. Little or no crit-
      ical commentary.

20   Delattre, F. LE ROMAN PSYCHOLOGIQUE DE VIRGINIA WOOLF.
      Paris, 1932.

21   Dölle, Erika. EXPERIMENT UND TRADITION IN DER PROSA VIRGINIA
      WOOLFS. Munchen: Fink, 1971.

22   Fink, I. VIRGINIA WOOLFS STELLUNG ZUR WIRKLICHKEIT. Marburg,
      1933.

23   Forster, E. M. VIRGINIA WOOLF. Cambridge, 1942. (Previously
      published in THE YALE REVIEW as "The Art of Virginia Woolf").

      A tribute by one of Virginia Woolf's best friends. An admir-
      able piece of balanced assessment. "She was a poet who at-
      tempted to write something as near to the novel as possible".
      Finds in Woolf's characterization her chief weakness as a
      novelist.

      REVIEWED:

      (a)   Bowen, Elizabeth. THE OBSERVER. Lond., June 14, 1942,
            p. 13.
      (b)   THE DURHAM UNIVERSITY JOURNAL. Durham, England, 4: 1,
            December 1942, p. 35.
      (c)   Column, Mary M. THE NEW YORK HERALD TRIBUNE. October
            4, 1942, p. 3.
      (d)   Burnham, David. THE COMMONWEAL. New York, October 2,
            1942, 567-68.
      (e)   THE TIMES LITERARY SUPPLEMENT. Lond., May 23, 1942, p.
            260.
      (f)   MacCarthy, Desmond. THE SUNDAY TIMES. June 14, 1942,
            p. 3.
      (g)   Schorer, Mark. THE YALE REVIEW. 32: 2, December 1942.

24   Gruber, Ruth. VIRGINIA WOOLF: A STUDY. Leipzig, 1935.

      The first full-length study of Virginia Woolf from Germany.
      Descriptive rather than evaluative. Discusses Woolf's lyr-
      ical psychology and her conception of time.

25   Guiguet, Jean. VIRGINIA WOOLF AND HER WORKS. Translated from
      the French by Jean Stewart. Lond., 1965.

      The most exhaustive and thoroughly documented study so far of
      Virginia Woolf by a French scholar. Gives a résumé of the

chief lines of criticism of Mrs. Woolf's works. Discusses her background and her purpose as a writer. Finds in all her books a common preoccupation--"the quest for reality which was none other than the content of moments of vision"--and the search for "the tools capable of expressing reality as she conceived it". Examines from this point of view such 'basic problems' in Virginia Woolf's novels as characterization, time and space, symbolism, structure and lyricism. Guiguet's main concern is to stress Virginia Woolf's continuous effort to find a form that would communicate her own awareness of life. Provides thorough and stimulating analyses of all the novels. A very well-documented book which draws often on quotations from Woolf's DIARY in support of its conclusions. Contains a useful bibliography of books and articles on Mrs. Woolf.

26   Hafley, James. THE GLASS ROOF: VIRGINIA WOOLF AS NOVELIST. Berkeley, California, 1954.

An illuminating critical study of Virginia Woolf by an American critic. Examines, in depth, the Bergsonian concepts of flux and durée in Virginia Woolf's novels.

27   Hawthorn, Jeremy. VIRGINIA WOOLF'S MRS. DALLOWAY: A STUDY IN ALIENATION. Sussex, England, 1975.

28   Holtby, Winifred. VIRGINIA WOOLF. Lond., 1932.

The first full-length study of Virginia Woolf during her lifetime. An appreciative estimate of her lyrical genius and her cinematographic technique. There is not much of evaluation and judgement.

REVIEWED:

(a)   Mitchison, Naomi. THE WEEK-END REVIEW. Lond., October 15, 1932, p. 447.
(b)   Macaulay, Rose. THE SPECTATOR. Lond., October 29, 1932, 585-86.
(c)   THE NEW STATESMAN AND NATION. Lond., April 16, 1932, p. 500.
(d)   THE TIMES LITERARY SUPPLEMENT. Lond., October 20, 1932, p. 755.
(e)   THE BOOKMAN. Lond., November 1932, p. 122.

29   Hungerford, E. A. THE NARROW BRIDGE OF ART: VIRGINIA WOOLF'S EARLY CRITICISM 1905-1925. Michigan, 1965.

30   Johnson, Manly. VIRGINIA WOOLF. New York, 1973.

"Johnson does a remarkably straightforward job of treating Woolf's celebrated experiments with literary technique,

her delicacy and sensitivity of style, her preoccupation with
time, death and psychology".

31   Johnstone, J. K.   THE BLOOMSBURY GROUP: A STUDY OF E. M.
      FORSTER, LYTTON STRACHEY, VIRGINIA WOOLF AND THEIR CIRCLE.
      Lond. and New York, 1954.

      An important study of Virginia Woolf's aesthetic philosophy.
      The focus is on the relation between Mrs. Woolf's conception
      of fiction, her view of time and personality and the Blooms-
      bury milieu.

      REVIEWED:

      (a)   Pritchett, V. S.   THE NEW YORK TIMES.   September 26,
            1954, 36-37.
      (b)   Muir, Edwin.   THE OBSERVER.   May 30, 1954, p. 9.
      (c)   Nicolson, Benedict.   THE NEW STATESMAN.   June 19, 1954.
      (d)   THE TIMES LITERARY SUPPLEMENT.   August 20, 1954.

32   Kelley, Alice Van Buren.   THE NOVELS OF VIRGINIA WOOLF: FACT
      AND VISION.   Chicago, 1973.

      "With plodding and meticulous thoroughness Alice Kelley traces
      the development of Cartesian dualism in the novels of Virginia
      Woolf.   In a cursory introduction Mrs. Kelley defines the
      dichotomy between fact and vision as a distinction between the
      'world of physical isolation and limitation' and 'the spiritual
      world of unity and pattern'.   She then proceeds to interpret
      Woolf's major fiction in antithetical terms and concludes that
      BETWEEN THE ACTS articulates a final Hegelian synthesis of po-
      larities."

33   Kettle, Arnold.   MRS. DALLOWAY.   Lond., 1973.

34   Latham, Jacqueline, S. M. (ed).   CRITICS ON VIRGINIA WOOLF
      (Readings in Literary Criticism).   Coral Gables, Florida,and
      London, 1970.

      Among the critics are David Daiches, Joan Bennett, M. C.
      Bradbrook, James Hafley, Jean Guiguet and A. D. Moody.

35   Leaska, Mitchell A.   VIRGINIA WOOLF'S TO THE LIGHTHOUSE: A
      STUDY IN CRITICAL METHOD.   Columbia and London, 1970.

      A detailed analysis of Virginia Woolf's technique in TO THE
      LIGHTHOUSE.   A careful examination of the novel's stylistics.
      Leaska's major concern is to demonstrate by a close textual
      study of TO THE LIGHTHOUSE how Virginia Woolf wanted to re-
      veal "the whole constellation of emotional and mental proc-
      esses which make up human experience".   For this purpose Woolf
      broke away from the conventional form of the novel and focused

on the shifting viewpoints of her characters.

36   Lohmüller, G. DIE FRAU IM WERK VIRGINIA WOOLFS. Leipzig,
      1937.

37   Love, J. O. WORLDS IN CONSCIOUSNESS: MYTHOPOETIC THOUGHT IN
      THE NOVELS OF VIRGINIA WOOLF. Berkeley, California, 1970.

38   Majumdar, Robin and McLaurin, Allen (eds.). VIRGINIA WOOLF:
      THE CRITICAL HERITAGE. Lond., 1975.

      The editors trace the reception of Woolf's work from her first
      novel, THE VOYAGE OUT (1915) until her death in 1941. The
      book contains a wide-ranging selection of British and American
      reviews which are preceded by a long critical introduction dis-
      cussing the various trends in Woolf criticism.

39   Marder, Herbert. FEMINISM AND ART: A STUDY OF VIRGINIA WOOLF.
      Chicago, 1968.

      One of the few studies which emphasize the social relevance
      of Woolf's novels. Also looks at her feminism from a new
      angle. Far from "pure" works of art Virginia Woolf's novels
      combine social criticism and art. The importance of feminine
      modes of thought in a male dominated society plays a key role
      in her fiction.

      "The subjugation of women and the suppression of feminine
      modes of thought are central facts of history and--accord-
      ing to Virginia Woolf --the source of most of our social and
      psychological disorders".

40   McLaurin, Allen. VIRGINIA WOOLF: THE ECHOES ENSLAVED.
      Lond., 1973.

      Discusses by thematic and structural analyses of Woolf's novels
      two major aspects of her art: 'repetition' and 'rhythm'.

41   Mcnichol, Stella (ed.). MRS. DALLOWAY'S PARTY: A SHORT STORY
      SEQUENCE BY VIRGINIA WOOLF. Lond., 1973.

      Mcnichol presents together for the first time the seven short
      stories in which the Dalloways and their party appear.

42   Moody, A. D. VIRGINIA WOOLF (Writers and Critics Series).
      Lond., 1968.

      A challenge to the SCRUTINY line of attack on Virginia Woolf's
      novels. Highlights the human value and contemporary meaning
      of Woolf's novels in a chaotic and disunified age of transition.
      Traces the development of Virginia Woolf's critical reputation
      in England.

43   Naremore, James. THE WORLD WITHOUT A SELF: VIRGINIA WOOLF

AND THE NOVEL. New Haven, Connecticut, 1974.

Continuing the line of Joan Bennett and others (See Nos. 7; 18), Naremore examines Virginia Woolf's novels against her perspective, and shows how her view of the world 'without a self', a world of fluidity and flux, influenced her fictional art.

44 Nathan, Monique. VIRGINIA WOOLF PAR ELLE MÊME. Paris, 1956.

45 Newton, Deborah. VIRGINIA WOOLF. Melbourne, 1946.

Contains short descriptive chapters on the individual novels.

46 Noble, John Russell (ed.). RECOLLECTIONS OF VIRGINIA WOOLF BY HER CONTEMPORARIES. London and New York, 1972.

REVIEWED:

Connolly, Cyril. THE SUNDAY TIMES. Lond., April 16, 1972, p. 35.

47 Pasternack, G. ASPEKTE DES KOMISCHEN BEI VIRGINIA WOOLF. Köln, 1962.

48 Pippett, Aileen. THE MOTH AND THE STAR: A BIOGRAPHY OF VIRGINIA WOOLF. Boston, 1955.

The first biography of Virginia Woolf. Deals with some of the important facts of her life: her delicate health, sensitive nature, association with Bloomsbury etc. Also shows the genesis and the various stages in the progress of Mrs. Woolf's books as revealed in her letters to her friend Victoria Sackville-West. These unpublished letters cast helpful light on many of Virginia Woolf's attitudes and opinions, her ideas and views on literature. Discusses Mrs. Woolf's books in their chronological order and relates them to her complex personality. Not much of critical analysis or evaluation of Virginia Woolf's work.

REVIEWED:

(a) Catherine W. McCul. AMERICA. New York, October 15, 1955, 76-77.
(b) Rumer Godden. THE NEW YORK HERALD TRIBUNE. September 1955, p. 3.
(c) Leon Edel. THE SATURDAY REVIEW OF LITERATURE. New York, September 24, 1955, 13-14.
(d) John R. Willingham. THE NATION. New York, November 19, 1955, p. 445.

(e) V. S. Pritchett. THE NEW YORK TIMES. September 25, 1955, p. 7.

49 Quennell, Peter. A LETTER TO MRS. WOOLF (Hogarth Letters No. 2). London, 1932.

50 Rantavaara, Irma. VIRGINIA WOOLF AND BLOOMSBURY. Helsinki, 1953.

Another thorough work for background study. Discusses Virginia Woolf's novels against the Cambridge intellectual milieu. A most comprehensive account of Bloomsbury. The approach is 'historical' rather than exclusively critical. Deals at length with Mrs. Woolf's chief characteristics: her aestheticism, meditative vision, and her passionate search for stability and order in the flux of life. Contains a useful bibliography of Virginia Woolf studies.

REVIEWED:

(a) Gifford, Henry. THE REVIEW OF ENGLISH STUDIES. Lond., Vol. 5, October 1954, 430-431.
(b) Harkness, Bruce. THE JOURNAL OF ENGLISH AND GERMANIC PHILOLOGY. Urbana, Illinois, Vol. LIII, No. 1, January 1954, 137-138.

51 Rey, Jean. THE EVOLUTION OF MRS. WOOLF'S TECHNIQUE AND STYLE. (Mémoire Présenté à la Faculté des Lettres de Lille).Paris, 1930.

52 Richter, Harvena. VIRGINIA WOOLF: THE INWARD VOYAGE. Princeton, 1970.

Shows how by her subjective methods Virginia Woolf "seeks to approximate the actual ways in which man sees, thinks and experiences time and change". A sound analysis of Woolf's craftsmanship. Appreciative without being adulatory.

53 Rillo, Lila E. KATHERINE MANSFIELD AND VIRGINIA WOOLF. Buenos Aires, 1944.

The Woolf-Mansfield relationship is discussed in terms of their common preoccupation with time and their search for the meaning of life.

54 Sanna, V. IL ROMANZO DI VIRGINIA WOOLF. Florence, 1951.

55 Schaefer, Josephine O'Brien. THE THREE-FOLD NATURE OF REALITY IN THE NOVELS OF VIRGINIA WOOLF (Studies in English Literature). The Hague, 1965.

"Virginia Woolf is aware of three aspects of human experience:

10

the experience of the natural; the experience of responsible
action; and the experience of the private life".

56 Sprague, Claire (ed.). VIRGINIA WOOLF: A COLLECTION OF
    CRITICAL ESSAYS. New Jersey, 1971.

57 Sugiyama, Yoku. RAINBOW AND GRANITE: A STUDY OF VIRGINIA
    WOOLF. Tokyo, 1973.

58 Thakur, N. C. THE SYMBOLISM OF VIRGINIA WOOLF. London and
    New York, 1965.

    Sees Virginia Woolf as a seer and a mystic. Examines the land-
    scape, atmosphere and characters of Woolf's novels in terms of
    her symbolic meaning.

59 Trautmann, Joanne. THE JESSAMY BRIDES: THE FRIENDSHIP OF VIR-
    GINIA WOOLF AND VICTORIA SACKVILLE-WEST   (Penn. State Studies).
    Pennsylvania, 1974.

    "An investigation of the influence of this friendship on the
    works of both writers".

60 Verga, Ines. VIRGINIA WOOLF'S NOVELS AND THEIR ANALOGY TO
    MUSIC. Buenos Aires, 1945.

    Throws interesting light on one important aspect of Woolf's
    structural pattern. Shows how her novels resemble music in
    their word-patterns, leitmotifs, etc.

61 Voglar, Thomas A. (comp). TWENTIETH CENTURY INTERPRETATIONS
    OF TO THE LIGHTHOUSE: A COLLECTION OF CRITICAL ESSAYS. New
    Jersey, 1970.

62 Weidner, E. IMPRESSIONISMUS UND EXPRESSIONISMUS IN DEN
    ROMANEN VIRGINIA WOOLFS. Greifswald, 1934.

63 Wiget, E. VIRGINIA WOOLF UND DIE KONZEPTION DER ZEIT IN IHREN
    WERKEN. Zurich, 1949.

64 Woodring, Carl. VIRGINIA WOOLF (Columbia Essays on Modern
    Writers). New York and London, 1966.

    A descriptive and chronological survey of Virginia Woolf's
    books.

II. ARTICLES ON VIRGINIA WOOLF

65   Aiken, Conrad. "The Novel as Work of Art", THE DIAL,
     Chicago, July 1927, 41-44.

     A major piece of Woolf criticism in America in the twenties.
     Praises Virginia Woolf's poetic style, but dislikes her 'so-
     phisticated aloofness' from the raw stuff of life. Mrs.
     Woolf's characters are, according to Aiken, "creatures of se-
     clusion, creatures of shelter."

66   Allen, Walter. "Between the Acts", READING A NOVEL. Lond.,
     1949, 40-43.

     Comments on the significance of Woolf's last novel: the un-
     ceasing continuity of life and the agony of the artist who
     fails to express his vision.

67   Ames, Kenneth J. "Elements of Mock-Heroic in Virginia Woolf's
     MRS. DALLOWAY", MODERN FICTION STUDIES, Lafayette, Indiana,
     18: Autumn 1972, 363-374.

     Discusses MRS. DALLOWAY against the 18th century concept of
     order and proportion in life and art, and shows how Woolf em-
     ploys some neo-classic devices in order to depict these ideals
     in Sir William Bradshaw.

68   Arauje, Victorade. "A Haunted House: The Shattered Glass",
     STUDIES IN SHORT FICTION, Newberry College, South Carolina,
     III: Winter 1966, 157-165.

69   Auden, W. H. "A Consciousness of Reality" (Rev. art), THE
     NEW YORKER, March 6, 1954, 99-104.

     Claims, unlike most critics, that Virginia Woolf unifies in
     herself a mystical vision of life with a "sense for the con-
     crete and the actual".

70   Auerbach, Erich. "The Brown Stocking", MIMESIS: THE REPRE-
     SENTATION OF REALITY IN WESTERN LITERATURE, translated by
     Willard R. Trask. Princeton, 1963, Chap. 2, 525-553.

     Argues, through a close analysis of the opening chapter of TO
     THE LIGHTHOUSE, that by reality Woolf meant not "the exterior
     objective reality" but the flow of consciousness released by
     external events. Stresses the close relation between her view
     of reality and her technique.

71   Bagnold, Enid. "Virginia", ADAM INTERNATIONAL REVIEW, Lond.,
     Vol. 37, 1972, p. 15.

     Describes her first meeting with Virginia Woolf.

72   Baker, Denys. "To The Lighthouse", JOHN O'LONDON'S WEEKLY,
     Lond., May 7, 1954, p. 461.

     About the significance of Cornwall in Virginia Woolf's TO THE
     LIGHTHOUSE.

73   Baker, Margaret. "Virginia Woolf", THE ADELPHI, Lond., May
     1941, 294-95.

     "For the first time Virginia Woolf was explaining exactly what
     went on inside a woman's brain".

74   Baldanza, Frank. "TO THE LIGHTHOUSE Again", PMLA, New York,
     Vol. 70, June 1955, 548-552.

     On the autobiographical interest of TO THE LIGHTHOUSE.
     Finds in Mr. and Mrs. Ramsay the prototypes of Virginia
     Woolf's father Sir Leslie Stephen and her mother Julia Stephen.
     The protest of Mr. Ramsay's children against his dogmatic at-
     titude is similar to that made by Sir Leslie's own children.

75   _____. "ORLANDO and the Sackvilles", PMLA, Vol.
     70, March 1955, 274-279.

     Stresses the link between ORLANDO and the other Woolf novels.
     All of them have a common preoccupation with personality, time
     and feminism.

76   _____. "Clarissa Dalloway's Party Consciousness",
     MODERN FICTION STUDIES, Lafayette, 1:1, February 1956, 24-30.

     The 'party', a key symbol in MRS. DALLOWAY, symbolizes Virginia
     Woolf's concept of reality which means for her "an inter-
     related series of states of mind".

77   Banti, A. "Umanitá della Woolf", PARAGONE, Florence, Italy,
     3: 1952.

78   Basham, C. "BETWEEN THE ACTS", DURHAM UNIVERSITY JOURNAL,
     Durham, England, Vol. LIII, No. 2, March 1960, 87-94.

     Remarks on the tone and technique of the novel. The predomin-
     ant mood of the book seems to the critic to be one of loneli-
     ness, isolation and disintegration.

79   Batchelor, J. B. "Feminism in Virginia Woolf", ENGLISH,
     Lond., Vol. XVII, No. 97, Spring 1968, 1-7.

     Throws new light on Woolf's feminism. Argues, unlike several
     other critics (see Nos. 1038; 1040), that Virginia Woolf does
     not plead for the feminists and their 'warrior' attitudes.
     What she insists on is the need for women to develop fully as
     individuals and as members of society and their co-operation
     with men to achieve a synthesis of feminine and masculine qual-

ities: the ideal of the androgynous mind (see Nos. 39; 79-80;
236 for a similar viewpoint).

80   Bazin, Nancy Toping. "Virginia Woolf's Quest for Equilib-
     rium", MODERN LANGUAGE QUARTERLY, Washington, Vol. 32, No.
     3, September 1971, 305-319.

     Another article on Woolf's concept of the androgynous human
     personality. All her novels, the critic maintains, affirm
     Mrs. Woolf's faith in the individuality and wholeness of human
     nature. This study sums up this central doctrine in Woolf's
     feminist cult.

81   Beach, J. W. "Virginia Woolf", THE ENGLISH JOURNAL, New York,
     Vol. XXVI, October 1938, 603-612.

     Represents one common complaint about Woolf's novels in the
     1930s: she is over-refined and has a feeble grasp on
     the external world.

82   Beaumont, Germaine. "Mrs. Brown ou l'Art du Roman", NOUVELLES
     LITTÉRAIRES, Paris, No. 185, February 21, 1963, pp. 1, 7.

83   Beck, Warren. "For Virginia Woolf", FORMS OF MODERN FICTION,
     ed. W. V. O'Connor, Minneapolis, 1948, 243-253.

     A powerful defence of the human worth of Woolf's novels in
     sharp contrast to the SCRUTINY and the Marxist viewpoints.

84   Beede, Margaret. "Virginia Woolf: Romantic", THE NORTH
     DAKOTA QUARTERLY, Grand Forks, North Dakota, Vol. 27, Winter
     1959, 21-29.

     Describes the resemblance between Virginia Woolf and the Eng-
     lish romantics.

85   Beja, Morris. "Matches Struck in the Dark: Virginia Woolf's
     Moments of Vision", THE CRITICAL QUARTERLY, Manchester, Vol.
     6, No. 2, Summer 1964, 137-152.

     A sound analysis of Virginia Woolf's technique. Clarifies
     the concept of the moments of vision in Woolf's novels.
     Thinks that the moments of vision are the bases of Virginia
     Woolf's art and they determine the character and especially
     the structure of her novels.

86   Beker, Miroslav. "London as a Principle of Structure in MRS.
     DALLOWAY", MODERN FICTION STUDIES, Lafayette, 18: 1972, 375-
     385.

     Shows how London reveals the novel's characters and prompts
     its action. "It is London that brings about the link between
     the characters and the scenes".

87   Bell, Barbara Currier and Ohmann, Carol. "Virginia Woolf's
      Criticism: A Polemical Preface", CRITICAL INQUIRY, Chicago,
      Vol. I, December 1974.

88   Bell, Clive. "Virginia Woolf", THE DIAL, Chicago, Vol.
      LXXVI, December 1924, 451-465.

      One of the earliest studies of Virginia Woolf's novels. The
      centre of focus is on the relation between Mrs. Woolf's vision
      and her form. This approach was a new trend in Woolf criticism.

89   Bell, M. "Virginia Woolf Now", MASSACHUSETTS REVIEW (Univer-
      sity of Massachusetts), Vol. 14, Autumn 1973, 655-687.

90   Bell, Quentin. "The Biographer, the Critic, and the Light-
      house" (Rev. art), ARIEL: A REVIEW OF INTERNATIONAL ENGLISH
      LITERATURE   (University of Calgary, Canada), 2:1, 1971, 94-
      101.

      Comments on the theme and method of TO THE LIGHTHOUSE. Thinks
      that Woolf's purpose in this novel was "to examine in the ut-
      most depth the conjugal and parental situation ... which made
      the happiness of her childhood, and which ... made a nightmare
      of her adolescence". Stresses the close relation between
      Woolf's technique and painting.

91   Benjamin, Anna S. "Towards an Understanding of the Meaning of
      Virginia Woolf's MRS. DALLOWAY", WISCONSIN STUDIES IN CONTEM-
      PORARY LITERATURE, Wisconsin, Vol. 6, No. 2, Summer 1963,
      214-217.

      Maintains that Woolf's 'organic' view of reality in MRS. DAL-
      LOWAY is the basis for her 'circular' as opposed to the 'lin-
      ear' method of presenting action and time.

      "... in representing a view of reality in which characters
      and nature interpenetrate and are part of an overwhelming
      continuity of time, in probing beneath the surface of action
      to the reality beneath, and in attacking the problem of what
      meaning can human life take on in the nexus of the organic
      world, Woolf adds enormous scope to the novel".

92   Bennett, Joan. "Virginia Woolf", THE CAMBRIDGE REVIEW, Cam-
      bridge, November 8, 1941, 69-70.

      As in her book (No. 7), Mrs. Bennett relates Virginia Woolf's
      work to her individual perspective.

93   _____. "Critics who Have Influenced Taste--IV Vir-
      ginia Woolf", THE TIMES, Lond., April 25, 1963, p. 15.

      Evaluates Woolf's position as a critic. Thinks that Virginia
      Woolf did not formulate any critical theories. Her principal
      characteristic as a literary critic was her capacity for ap-

preciation and enjoyment, and she "increased this capacity" in others.

94 _____. "Le Journal inédit de Virginia Woolf", ROMAN, Paris, January 1951, 6-8.

95 Bevis, Dorothy. "THE WAVES: A Fusion of symbol, style and thought in Virginia Woolf", TWENTIETH CENTURY LITERATURE, Denver, Colorado, 2: April 1956, 5-19.

"The incomprehensible nature" of human life is the theme of Virginia Woolf's THE WAVES, and she has "expressed it in the thought, inscribed it in the words, drawn it in the pictures, and fused it into a whole".

96 Bishop, Morchard. "Towards a Biography of FLUSH", TIMES LIT-ERARY SUPPLEMENT, London, December 15, 1966, 118.

Points out some historical inaccuracies in Virginia Woolf's FLUSH.

97 Blanchard, Margaret. "Socialization in MRS. DALLOWAY", COL-LEGE ENGLISH, Chicago, 34: 2, November 1972, 287-307.

Marxist interpretation of Woolf's work, but the attitude is more favourable than that in other Marxist criticisms (See Nos. 130; 528). "What is impressive about Virginia Woolf is how she evolved from her inherited class complacency to a feminist position which attempted to bridge the gap between working and middle class women. She examined the economic bases of women's oppression".

98 Blanche, Jacques-Emile. "Un nouveau roman de Virginia Woolf", LES NOUVELLES LITTÉRAIRES, Paris, February 16, 1929, p. 9.

99 _____. "Entretien avec Virginia Woolf", LES NOUVEL-LES LITTÉRAIRES, Paris, August 13, 1927, 1-2.

100 Blotner, Joseph. "Mythic Patterns in TO THE LIGHTHOUSE", PMLA, New York, Vol. 71, No. 4, September 1956, 547-562.

Interprets TO THE LIGHTHOUSE in terms of the Kore and the Oedipus myths and thinks that the novel's characters and situations can be seen in relation to each other within the framework of these myths. The approach is mainly psycho-analytical.

101 Borgal, Clement. "Virginia Woolf ou le point de Vue de Sirius", CRITIQUE, Paris, No. 158, July 1960, 609-614.

102 Bowen, Elizabeth. "The Achievement of Virginia Woolf" (Rev. art.), NEW YORK TIMES BOOK REVIEW, January 26, 1949, 1-21. Reprinted in Bowen, COLLECTED IMPRESSIONS, Lond., 1950.

Thinks that Virginia Woolf was "essentially a creature of her environment and her time", and she "affected the consciousness of the age in which she wrote".

103   Boyd, Elizabeth F. "Luriana, Lurilee", NOTES & QUERIES, Lond., Oct. 1963, 380-381.

Traces the source of the poem "Luriana, Lurilee" which Virginia Woolf quotes in TO THE LIGHTHOUSE.

104   Brace, Marjorie. "Worshipping Solid Objects: The Pagan World of Virginia Woolf" (Rev. article), ACCENT ANTHOLOGY, ed. Kerker Quinn and C. Shattuck, New York, 1946, pp. 489-495.

The chief merit of the article lies in the conclusion that "an excess of moral sensibility and humaneness rather than an aesthetic aloofness" caused Virginia Woolf to move away from the world of social reality. "To her the unknowableness of people and the impossibilities of communion were ... terrifying".

105   Bradbrook, Frank W. "Virginia Woolf: The Theory and Practice of Fiction", THE PELICAN GUIDE TO ENGLISH LITERATURE, Vol. 7, ed. Boris Ford, Lond., 1967, pp. 257-269.

An attack on Woolf's fiction along the SCRUTINY lines. Asserts that Mrs. Woolf's conception of fiction as a record of "innumerable atoms" of experience is unsatisfactory, because she fails to discriminate between the significance and values of the various experiences.

106   Bradbrook, M. C. "Notes on the style of Mrs. Woolf", SCRUTINY, Cambridge, Vol. I, May 1932, pp. 33-38.

One of the most classic instances of the SCRUTINY case against Virginia Woolf. Dr. Bradbrook condemns Woolf's subjective and lyrical approach to the novel. Complains that she is unable to present clearly defined situations and to delineate solid and objective characters. What one finds in her novels is mere "sensation in the void" with no co-ordinated structure, no clear attitude to life.

107   Brewster, D. and Burnell, A. "The Wild Goose: Virginia Woolf's Pursuit of Life", ADVENTURE OR EXPERIENCE, New York, 1930, 77-116.

108   Brogan, Howard. "Science and Narrative Structure in Austen, Hardy and Woolf", NINETEENTH CENTURY FICTION, California, Vol. 2, No. 4, March 1957, 276-287.

Believes that Virginia Woolf's narrative structure was related to certain scientific concepts of her time, the primary one being the idea of relativity.

109   Brooke, B. G. "Virginia Woolf", THE NINETEENTH CENTURY &
       AFTER, Lond., Vol. 130, December 1941, 334-340.

       Discusses the influence of the post-impressionist painters
       on Woolf's aesthetic theory.

110   Brower, Reuben A. "The Novel as Poem: Virginia Woolf Ex-
       ploring a Critical Metaphor", THE INTERPRETATION OF NARRATIVE:
       THEME AND PRACTICE, ed. Morton W. Bloomfield (Harvard English
       Studies I), Harvard, 1970, 229-247.

       Shows by an analysis of the opening passage of TO THE LIGHT-
       HOUSE how "the saturation of images and rhythmic pulsations"
       bring the novel closer to lyrical poetry.

111   _____. "Something central which permeated Virginia
       Woolf and MRS. DALLOWAY", THE FIELDS OF LIGHT: AN EXPERIMENT
       IN CRITICAL READING, New York, 1951, Chap. VII, 123-127.

       Provides a new insight into Virginia Woolf's technique in
       MRS. DALLOWAY. Maintains that what holds the novel's frag-
       mentary experiences together is not any coherent logical
       plot, but "a metaphorical nucleus" which is sustained by the
       use of recurrent symbolic metaphors, images and words.

112   Brown, Robert Curtis. "Laurence Sterne and Virginia Woolf:
       A Study in Literary Continuity", THE UNIVERSITY OF KANSAS
       CITY REVIEW, Kansas City, Missouri, Vol. 26, No. 2, December
       1959, 153-159.

       About Sterne's influence on Virginia Woolf--the free associ-
       ation of ideas, emphasis on subjective reactions, and belief
       in the mind instead of the clock time.

113   Bryher. "A Good Pasture Needs Many Glasses" (Rev. art.), LIFE
       AND LETTERS TODAY, Lond., September 1941, 195-197.

       A powerful defence of the human value of Virginia Woolf's
       work. Argues that "it is never remoteness but inability to
       escape the universal suffering of humanity that is the prev-
       alent feature in Virginia Woolf's writings".

114   Bullett, Gerald. "Virginia Woolf", THE ENGLISH JOURNAL, New
       York, Vol. XVIII, No. 1, December 1928, 73-30.

       A general consideration of Virginia Woolf's novels up to TO
       THE LIGHTHOUSE.

115   Burgum, E. B. "Virginia Woolf and the Empty Room", THE NOVEL
       AND THE WORLD'S DILEMMA, New York, 1947, Chap. 8, 120-139.

       Discusses one major motif in Woolf's work: the problem of
       disintegration and the need for satisfying human relation-
       ships.

116   Burnham, David. "The Intellectual Lady of Bloomsbury" (Rev.
       art.), THE COMMONWEAL, New York, October 2, 1942, 567-568.

       Defends Virginia Woolf's fictional art. Maintains that in-
       stead of limiting the art of the novel, Virginia Woolf did,
       in fact, expand it. She discovered a valid substitute for
       the creation of memorable characters and the depiction of
       temporal action.

117   Burra, Peter. "Virginia Woolf", THE NINETEENTH CENTURY,
       Lond., Vol. CXV, January 1934, 112-125.

       Examines, among other things, the influence of contemporary
       psychology on Virginia Woolf.

118   Carew, Dudley. "Virginia Woolf", THE LONDON MERCURY, CCCXXX,
       May 1926, 40-49. Published previously in LIVING AGE,CCCXXX,
       1926, 47-54.

       Repeats one of the most common complaints about Woolf's fic-
       tion: its lack of robust characters. "Instead of being the
       live vivid actors, her characters are little more than
       dangling puppets".

119   Cazamian, L. "La philosophie de Virginia Woolf", ÉTUDES
       ANGLAISES, Paris, 5, 1952.

120   Cecil, David. "Virginia Woolf", POETS AND STORY TELLERS,
       Lond., 1949, 160-180.

       A typical example of the anti-aesthetic line of attack on
       Virginia Woolf's novels. Regards Woolf as primarily an
       aesthete who is preoccupied with the inner life of the in-
       dividual. "A novel without drama, without moral values, and
       without character and strong personal emotion in it is a hard
       thing to write and it cannot be said that Virginia Woolf is
       always successful".

121   Chapman, Robert T. "The Lady in the Looking-Glass: Modes of
       Perception in a short story by Virginia Woolf", MODERN FIC-
       TION STUDIES, Lafayette, Indiana, 18: April 1972, 331-337.

       Explains the concept of truth and reality in Woolf's fiction.
       "The act of perception involves a continual organization of
       sense data" and "the mind translates external facts into sub-
       jective knowlege". The process is described in the story THE
       LADY IN THE LOOKING-GLASS.

122   Chastaing, Maxime. "Virginia Woolf et la Conscience
       Réfléchissante", JOURNAL DE PSYCHOLOGIE, Paris, Vol. 35, 1938-
       1939, 617-23.

123   Chattopadhyaya, Sisir: "Virginia Woolf and the Capture of
       'The Moment'", TECHNIQUE OF THE MODERN ENGLISH NOVEL, Calcutta,

1959, pp. 168-215.

Traces the development of Virginia Woolf's technique from
JACOB'S ROOM to BETWEEN THE ACTS and discusses the relevance
of her technical innovations to her conception of life.

124   Church, Margaret. "Concepts of Time in the Novels of Virginia
       Woolf and Aldous Huxley", MODERN FICTION STUDIES, Lafayette,
       Indiana, Vol. I, No. 2, May 1955, pp. 19-24.

Discusses Woolf's philosophy of time in Bergsonian terms.
Compares Virginia Woolf's view of time with that of Huxley.
Thinks that Mrs. Woolf follows the Bergsonian concept of du-
ration whereas Huxley rejects it. Gives illustrations from
JACOB'S ROOM, THE WAVES, THOSE BARREN LEAVES and TIME MUST
HAVE A STOP.

125   Cohn, Ruby. "Art in TO THE LIGHTHOUSE", MODERN FICTION
       STUDIES, Lafayette, Indiana, Vol. VIII, No. 2, Summer 1962,
       pp. 127-136.

Thinks that the key idea of the novel is the relationship between art and life--their duality and synthesis. Lily
Briscoe symbolises this function.

126   Collet, G. P. "Jacques-Emile Blanche and Virginia Woolf",
       COMPARATIVE LITERATURE, Eugene, Oregon, Vol. 17, No. 1, Win-
       ter 1965, 73-81.

Quotes the correspondence between Virginia Woolf and Jacques-
Emile Blanche about TO THE LIGHTHOUSE, MRS. DALLOWAY, ORLANDO
and THE WAVES.

127   Colum, Mary. "Woman as Artist", BOOK OF MODERN CATHOLIC
       PROSE, ed. T. Maynard, New York, 1928, 308-316. Originally
       published as a review of TO THE LIGHTHOUSE in the NEW YORK
       HERALD TRIBUNE, May 8, 1927, 1-6.

Makes the significant suggestion that Virginia Woolf was
temperamentally more akin to the 18th century than to any
other age--"partly critical, partly philosophical, highly
imaginative ... incapable of vaster emotions".

128   Conn, Peter. "Woolf's MRS. DALLOWAY", EXPLICATOR, Richmond,
       Virginia, Vol. 30, No. 1, September 1971, item 2.

Thinks that the four items Miss Kilman selects in the Army and
Navy Stores--hams, drugs, flowers, stationery--are closely related to the novel's action both imagistically and thematical-
ly.

129   Corsa, Helen Storm. "TO THE LIGHTHOUSE: Death, Mourning and
       Transfiguration", LITERATURE AND PSYCHOLOGY, New York, XXI, 3,
       1971, 115-131.

Psychological approach. Discusses in Freudian terms how the "whole novel in its pattern and movement evokes, recreates and delineates the mourning process".

130   Cowley, Malcolm. "Virginia Woolf's England under Glass" (Rev. art.), THE NEW REPUBLIC, New York, October 6, 1941, p. 440. Reprinted in his THINK BACK ON US, Carbondale, 1967.

A Marxist reaction to Woolf's work: "The outside world has made itself real to us as it never has to the people in her novels".

131   Cox, C. B. "Mental Image and the Style of Virginia Woolf", CRITICAL SURVEY, Manchester, V: 3, 1968, 205-208. Discusses the significance of the underwater images in TO THE LIGHT-HOUSE. They convey the intuition of Mrs. Ramsay: the 'mysterious region of life below the surface of consciousness'.

132   _____. "The Solitude of Virginia Woolf", THE FREE SPIRIT: A STUDY OF LIBERAL HUMANISM IN THE NOVELS OF GEORGE ELIOT, HENRY JAMES, E. M. FORSTER, VIRGINIA WOOLF, ANGUS WILSON, Lond., 1963, 103-116. Published in a slightly different form in THE CRITICAL QUARTERLY, Manchester, 1: 4, Winter 1959, 329-334.

Complains that "the weakness of Virginia Woolf's art is that she understood so little of human character ... her insistence on the value of sensitivity ignores the powerful loves and hates of ordinary people. She creates a narrow elite, and her failure to look outside this world is one reason why she is not a great novelist".

133   Craig, Patricia. "Virginia Woolf: The Simmering Darkness", THE OBSERVER (Colour Supplement), Lond., March 28, 1971, 16-20.

About Virginia Woolf's depression. Chiefly biographical.

134   Cumings, Melinda Feldt. "NIGHT AND DAY: Virginia Woolf's Visionary Synthesis of Reality", MODERN FICTION STUDIES, Lafayette, Indiana, 18: Autumn 1972, 339-349.

"NIGHT AND DAY ... deserves study in any account of Virginia Woolf's fiction which considers the primary tension in her art between the visionary moment and the matrix of material reality out of which it is generated".

135   Dahl, Liisa. "The Attributive Sentence Structure in the Stream of Consciousness Technique with Special Reference to the Interior Monologue used by Virginia Woolf, James Joyce and Eugene O'Neill", NEUPHILOLOGISCHE MITTEILUNGEN, Helsinki, Finland, LXVIII, 1967, 440-454.

Examines Woolf's use of sentences in relation to the stream

of consciousness technique. Mainly of linguistic interest.

136   . "Linguistic Features of the Stream of Consciousness Techniques of James Joyce, Virginia Woolf, and
Eugene O'Neill", ANNALES UNIVERSITATIS, Turku, Finland , 1970,
1-75.

"Virginia Woolf's stream of consciousness is clothed in a
language whose syntax and lexicon are for the most part conventional. Woolf's sentences are frequently 'impressionistic', tending to recreate landscape and atmosphere".

137 Daiches, David. "Virginia Woolf", THE NOVEL AND THE MODERN
WORLD, Chicago, 1939, 158-187.

One of the best studies of Woolf's art. Argues that the disintegration and instability of her time led Virginia Woolf to
abstract and to refine life, and the result was "something between lyrical poetry and fiction". Contains a brilliant analysis of MRS. DALLOWAY.

138   . "Virginia Woolf" (Rev. art.), THE TWENTIETH
CENTURY, Lond., December 1953.

One of the few studies of Virginia Woolf which highlight her
contemporary significance: "Virginia Woolf saw that the central fact about modern sensibility concerned the relation between personality and contact, between loneliness and love,
and this was more than most managed to see".

139 Daniel-Rops, H. "Une Technique Nouvelle: Le Monologue
Intérieur", CORRESPONDANT, Paris, January 25, 1932.

140 Détaller, Roger. "Mr. Lawrence and Mrs. Woolf", ESSAYS IN
CRITICISM, Lond., Vol. VIII, No. 1, January 1958, 48-59.

Disagrees with Woolf's opinion that Lawrence's style is
clumsy and slipshod. Maintains that Lawrence could handle
words as "effectively" as Mrs. Woolf.

141 Deiman, W. J. "History, Pattern, and Continuity in Virginia
Woolf", CONTEMPORARY LITERATURE, Madison, Wisconsin, 15, Winter 1974, 49-66.

142 Delattre, Floris. "Un Roman lyrique: THE WAVES", IMPRES-
SIONS, Paris, 5: Jan-Feb. 1938 /Special No. on Virginia
Woolf/.

143   . "La Durée Bergsonienne dans le Roman de
Virginia Woolf", REVUE ANGLO-AMÉRICAINE, Paris, 91: December
1931, 97-108.

Discusses, in detail, the similarity between Virginia Woolf's
view of time and that of Bergson. Thinks that the conception

of duration is at the very root of the novels of Virginia Woolf.

144 _____. "Le nouveau Roman de Virginia Woolf" (THE YEARS), ÉTUDES ANGLAISES, Paris, 1: July 1937, 289-96.

145 Delord, J. "Virginia Woolf's Critical Essays", REVUE DES LANGUES VIVANTES, Brussels, 29: 1963, 126-131.

146 Derbyshire, S. E. "An Analysis of Mrs. Woolf's TO THE LIGHTHOUSE", COLLEGE ENGLISH, Illinois, III, January 1942, 353-360.

Shows how TO THE LIGHTHOUSE moves round the Time-Death-Personality nexus.

147 Deurbergue, Jean. "Pour une rhétorique du récit romanesque: L'exemple de MRS. DALLOWAY", RECHERCHES ANGLAISES ET AMÉRICAINES, Paris, 4: 1971, 157-71.

148 Doner, Dean. "Virginia Woolf: The Service of Style", MODERN FICTION STUDIES, Lafayette, Indiana, Vol. II, No. I, February 1956, 1-12.

A useful viewpoint on the structural organization of Woolf's fiction. Maintains that although one does not find in Mrs. Woolf a chronological sequence of incidents as in the traditional novel, one nevertheless sees in her fiction a narrative pattern. This structure is not temporal but is developed through symbols. Mrs. Woolf extends her symbols to a variety of contexts and they serve to develop the novel's meaning. There is, therefore, no lack of progression and movement although it is not on the objective plane.

149 Dottin, Paul. "Les Sortilèges de Mrs. Virginia Woolf", REVUE DE FRANCE, Paris, April 1930, 556-566.

Qualified praise for Virginia Woolf's novels. Expresses reservations about her indirect style.

150 Elkan, L. "Virginia Woolf: Ihre Künstlerische Idee und Ihre Auffassung der Frau." Der Kreis, Hamburg, 8: 1931.

151 Empson, William. "Virginia Woolf", SCRUTINIES BY VARIOUS WRITERS, Lond., ed. E. Rickword, Vol. 2, 1931, pp. 204-216.

A close textual study of TO THE LIGHTHOUSE and a fine example of technical criticism. Praises Mrs. Woolf's sensitiveness but disapproves of her impressionist method. "It is the business of art to provide candelabra, to aggregate its matches into a lighthouse of many candlepower", and this is what Mrs. Woolf fails to do.

152 Enright, D. J. "To the Lighthouse or To India?", THE APOTH-

ECARY'S SHOP: ESSAYS ON LITERATURE, Lond., 1957, pp. 168-186.

A piece of hostile criticism mainly along SCRUTINY lines. Asserts that Forster's A PASSAGE TO INDIA is much more solidly constructed and closely linked to the outside world than Virginia Woolf's TO THE LIGHTHOUSE. The comparison also shows that Mrs. Woolf's characters are fragile and lifeless spirits. "Her people seem never to have lived, if to live means something more than feeling and thinking within the bounds of educated good taste".

153   Fischer, Gretl Kraus. "Edward Albee and Virginia Woolf", DALHOUSIE REVIEW, Halifax, Nova Scotia, XLIX, 1969, 196-207.

"Albee applies to the stage that combination of realism and delicate symbolism which such writers as James, Conrad, Joyce and Woolf brought to their novels and stories".

154   Fishman, Soloman. "Virginia Woolf on the Novel", SEWANEE REVIEW, Sewanee, LX, 1943, 321-340.

Thinks that Woolf's approach to the novel is neither entirely aesthetic nor exclusively utilitarian or moralistic. She stressed "the fusion of life and something that is not life ... rather than the differences which separate art and life".

155   Fleishman, Avrom. "Woolf and McTaggart", E.L.H. (Journal of English Literary History), Baltimore, Maryland, December 1969, 719-738.

Interprets Woolf's work in terms of some of the basic concepts of McTaggart's philosophy.

156   Forster, E. M. "The Novels of Virginia Woolf", THE YALE REVIEW, New Haven, Vol. XV, No. 3, April 1926, 505-514, reptd. in his ABINGER HARVEST, 1936.

A candid assessment of Woolf by one of her best friends. Thinks that she made 'a definite contribution' to the English novel by her power to convey 'the actual process of thinking'. But finds her characterization inadequate and unsatisfactory. Her characters do not 'live'.

157   _____. "The Art of Virginia Woolf", THE ATLANTIC MONTHLY, Boston, September 1942, 82-90, reptd. in his TWO CHEERS FOR DEMOCRACY, Lond., 1951.

A critical survey of Woolf's work. Maintains that her talents were those of a poet rather than those of a novelist. "She is a poet who wants to write something as near to a novel as possible".

158   Fortin, Rene E. "Sacramental Imagery in MRS. DALLOWAY",

24

RENASCENCE: ESSAYS ON VALUES IN LITERATURE (Published by Marquette University), XVIII: 1, Autumn 1965, 23-31.

Thinks that the imagery of MRS. DALLOWAY "suggests that the central action of the heroine is to find an adequate substitute for Christianity, and specifically for the sacramental sense of reality which is fostered".

159   Fox, S. D. "The Fish Pond as Symbolic Center in BETWEEN THE ACTS", MODERN FICTION STUDIES, 18: Autumn 1972, 467-473.

A perceptive study of the novel's structure. Unlike many critics who maintain that Woolf's novels are shapeless and disjointed, Fox shows how Mrs. Woolf secures unity--both structural and thematic--through symbols. "... every level in BETWEEN THE ACTS is attached metaphorically to the pond until it becomes a complex microcosm of persons, events, themes".

160   _____. "'An Unwritten Novel' and A Hidden Protagonist", VIRGINIA WOOLF QUARTERLY, San Diego, California, 4, Summer 1973, 69-77.

161   Francis, Herbert E. "Virginia Woolf and The Moment", THE EMORY UNIVERSITY QUARTERLY, Atlanta, Georgia, Vol. 16, 1960, 139-151.

"The moment is the key to her work, for in it the character experiences that illumination which gives meaning to life".

162   Franks, Gabriel. "Virginia Woolf and the Philosophy of G. E. Moore", THE PERSONALIST, California, Vol. L, No. 2, Spring 1969, 222-240.

Sees Virginia Woolf against the philosophical background. Maintains that Virginia Woolf's minute examination of human relationships was influenced by her study of Moore's PRINCIPIA ETHICA.

163   Fremantle, Anne. "And the Bush Was Not Consumed", THE COMMONWEAL, New York, Vol. LXIII, No. 3, November 2, 1945, 71-74.

General praise for Virginia Woolf's work. Claims that she was "tremendously successful" in her use of the novel as "an extension of consciousness".

164   Freedman, Ralph. "Awareness and Fact: The Lyrical Vision of Virginia Woolf", THE LYRICAL NOVEL: STUDIES IN HERMANN HESSE, ANDRE GIDE, AND VIRGINIA WOOLF, Princeton, New Jersey, 1963, 185-270.

Argues against the opinion that Virginia Woolf's novels are solipsistic. She attempted to combine both inner and outer experience, both "private awareness" and "external facts".

165 Friedman, Norman. "The Waters of Annihilation: Double Vision in TO THE LIGHTHOUSE", E.L.H., Baltimore, Maryland, Vol. XXII, No. 1, March 1955, 61-79.

Argues that the different movements and patterns of TO THE LIGHTHOUSE become intelligible to us only when they are related to a dual perspective: "subjective involvement" in and "objective detachment" from the flux of life. The water imagery symbolizes the transition from the single perspective to the "double vision which apprehends the nature of reality simultaneously from both points of view".

166 Fromm, Harold. "TO THE LIGHTHOUSE: Music and Sympathy", ENGLISH MISCELLANEY, Rome, XIX, 1968, 181-195.

"The final effect of the book is emotional in the way that music is emotional: the main contrasts and apprehensions are intuited clearly enough by a careful reader to enable him to feel the powerful emotional climax even if he cannot experience intellectually what the book has been about ... Mrs. Ramsay's greatness came from being able to experience the universal human experiences along with other people. And in so far as Virginia Woolf is an artist, she has been able to achieve that act of sympathy in the reader".

167 Gamble, Isabel. "The Secret Sharer in MRS. DALLOWAY", ACCENT, Illinois, Vol. XVI, No. 4, Autumn 1956, 235-251.

On the Woolf-Conrad relationship. Shows the affinity between Woolf's MRS. DALLOWAY and Conrad's THE SECRET SHARER in their "absorption in the mystery of the self" as well as in their technique.

168 Garnett, David. "Virginia Woolf", THE AMERICAN SCHOLAR, New York, Vol. 34, No. 3, Summer 1965, 371-386.

A general account of Virginia Woolf's life and work. Thinks that for Mrs. Woolf each person was "an individual with a secret" and to catch this secret was her chief aim.

169 Gelfant, Blanche H. "Love and Conversion in MRS. DALLOWAY", CRITICISM: A QUARTERLY FOR LITERATURE AND THE ARTS, Wayne State University, Detroit, Vol. 8, Winter 1966, pp. 229-245.

Argues that it is the conflict between love and conversion--the clash between the creative and destructive forces--which provides the thematic and structural unity in MRS. DALLOWAY. The characters who symbolize love and creativity such as Mrs. Dalloway and Septimus Warren Smith are pitted against those who stand for domination and conversion such as Dr. Holmes and William Bradshaw and Miss Kilman. And it is this polarity on which both the novel's theme and its structure are based.

170 Gennari, Genevieve. "La Littérature au feminin", NOUVELLES
     LITTÉRAIRES, Paris, 1, 7, 16 April, 1970.

171 German, Howard and Kaehele, Sharon. "The Dialectic of Time
     in ORLANDO", COLLEGE ENGLISH, Chicago, Illinois, Vol. 24, No.
     1, October 1962, pp. 35-41.

     ORLANDO illustrates "the individual's attempt to resolve the
     conflict between the forces of brevity and diuturnity ... the
     dialectic between the ephemeral and the enduring".

172 Ghiselin, Brewster. "Virginia Woolf's Party", THE SEWANEE
     REVIEW, Sewanee, Vol. LXXX, No. 1, Winter 1972, pp. 47-50.

     Argues that MRS. DALLOWAY is Virginia Woolf's answer to the
     question: Who sees truly? It is Clarissa Dalloway alone who
     "sees truly", because her understanding is "intuitive and
     imaginative". "Her party brings together the lonely, in a
     lonely communion transcending loneliness itself".

173 Gillen, Francis. "I am This, I am That: Shifting Distance
     and Movement in MRS. DALLOWAY", STUDIES IN THE NOVEL (North
     Texas State University), 4:3, Fall 1972, 484-493.

     In MRS. DALLOWAY the reader is aware of "the dangers and the
     necessity of a private sensibility". Shows how Clarissa's
     identification with Septimus "represents her rejection of her
     absolute dependence on society and on external stimulation.
     On the other hand, Septimus's rejection of society is also an
     absolute extreme".

174 Gillet, Louis. "L'ORLANDO de Mme Virginia Woolf", REVUE DES
     DEUX MONDES, Paris, Vol. 53, 1929, 218-230.

175 Goetach, Paul. "A Source of Mr. Bennett and Mrs. Brown",
     ENGLISH FICTION IN TRANSITION, Lafayette, Indiana, Vol. 7,
     No. 3, 1964, p. 168.

     Maintains that Arnold Bennett himself had realized his limit-
     ations as early as 1910, and so it was not fair of Virginia
     Woolf to use Bennett's self-criticism against him in 1924.

176 Goldman, Mark. "Virginia Woolf and the Critic as Reader",
     PMLA, New York, 80: June 1965, 275-284.

     Argues that Virginia Woolf's criticism is not merely impres-
     sionistic. Mrs. Woolf's aim is to combine "reason and emo-
     tion, sense and sensibility, the individual critic and the
     impersonal method".

177 _____. "Virginia Woolf and E. M. Forster: A Crit-
     ical Dialogue", TEXAS STUDIES IN LITERATURE AND LANGUAGE,
     Austin, Texas, 7: 1966, 387-400.

178   Gorsky, Susan.   "The Central Shadow: Characterization in
       THE WAVES", MODERN FICTION STUDIES, Lafayette, Indiana,
       18: Autumn 1972, 449-466.

       "The characters /of Virginia Woolf/ are individuals, but
       they are also a part of a larger community. The characters
       exist not simply at one level, but are one and yet separate,
       archetypal, representative and individual".

179   Graham, J. W.   "A Negative Note on Bergson and Virginia
       Woolf", ESSAYS IN CRITICISM, Lond., Vol. 6, No. 1, January
       1956, pp. 70-74.

       A new attitude to the Woolf-Bergson relationship. Thinks
       that despite Mrs. Woolf's interest in the Bergsonian concept
       of intuition, she was never greatly influenced by his basic
       ideas. Her conception of reality was different from his.
       She stressed its "fixity and permanence" while he looked up-
       on it as the "continual elaboration of the absolutely now".

180   _____. "Time in the Novels of Virginia Woolf",
       THE UNIVERSITY OF TORONTO QUARTERLY, Toronto, Vol. XVIII,
       January 1949, pp. 186-201.

       A perceptive analysis of Virginia Woolf's novels from the
       time-space angle. Focuses attention on the dichotomy be-
       tween two kinds of time: 'linear time' and 'mind time'.

181   _____. "The Caricature Value of Parody and Fan-
       tasy in ORLANDO", THE UNIVERSITY OF TORONTO QUARTERLY, Vol.
       XXX, No. 4, July 1961, pp. 345-366.

       "Through caricature Virginia Woolf explores in ORLANDO the
       argument that the novel must learn to fuse three things:
       its traditional power to render the texture of life closely;
       the freedom, detachment, and impersonality of poetry; and
       the concentration and strict control of drama. Her ironic
       detachment manifests itself on the one hand in parody and on
       the other in fantasy".

182   _____. "Point of View in THE WAVES: Some Services
       of the Style", THE UNIVERSITY OF TORONTO QUARTERLY, Vol. 39,
       No. 3, April 1970, 193-211.

       Maintains that in THE WAVES Virginia Woolf found her 'estab-
       lished method'--the presence of the author as narrator--in-
       adequate and used, instead, "certain features of a first per-
       son narrative".

183   _____. "Editing a Manuscript: Virginia Woolf's
       THE WAVES", EDITING TWENTIETH CENTURY TEXTS, ed. F. G. Hal-
       penny, Toronto, 1972, 77-92.

184   Graves, Nora C. "The Case of MRS. DALLOWAY", VIRGINIA

WOOLF QUARTERLY, San Diego, California, 1:3, Spring 1973, 51-59.

185   Green, David Bonnell. "ORLANDO and the Sackvilles", PMLA, New York, Vol. LXXI, No. 1, March 1956, 268-269.

Shows the connection between Orlando's change of sex and the change in the family line of the Sackvilles from the male to the female.

186   Griffin, Howard. "Virginia Woolf", THE SATURDAY REVIEW OF LITERATURE, New York, June 8, 1946, p. 14.

A poetic tribute to Virginia Woolf.

187   Grigson, Geoffrey. "Virginia Woolf and Henry Newbolt", THE BOOKMAN, Lond., November 1932, 121-122.

A brief comparison of the two writers. Declares that Virginia Woolf writes for the sophisticated audience whereas Henry Newbolt addresses the "Lower Fourth".

188   Guidi, A. "Spender, Praz e Virginia Woolf", LETTERATURA E ARTE CONTEMPORANEA, 2: 1951.

189   Guiguet, Jean. "La biographie de Virginia Woolf par Quentin Bell", ÉTUDES ANGLAISES, Paris, 26: 1973, 331-337.

190   _____. "Virginia Woolf devant la Critique" (Rev. art.), ÉTUDES ANGLAISES, Paris, 26: 1973, 338-345.

191   Hafley, James. "A Reading of BETWEEN THE ACTS", ACCENT, Illinois, XIII: 3, Summer 1953, 178-187.

Discusses the novel against its philosophical perspective. Relates it to the Bergsonian concepts of "free will" and "pure time". BETWEEN THE ACTS is "a novel about free will".

192   _____. "A Message for the Hounds" (Rev. art.), ACCENT, Illinois, Spring 1954, 156-159.

Asserts that Virginia Woolf's work is "solid" and does mean "something".

193   _____. "On One of Virginia Woolf's Short Stories" MODERN FICTION STUDIES, Lafayette, 11: 1, February 1956, 12-16.

Discusses how in its emphasis on moments of vision, the short story "Moments of Being" anticipates the technique of Virginia Woolf's later novels.

194   Haight, Gordon S. "Virginia Woolf" (Rev. art.), YALE REVIEW, New Haven, Connecticut, 62: 1973, 426-431.

195   Hale, Nancy. "Half-Glimpses of Genius" (Rev. art.), VIRGINIA QUARTERLY REVIEW, 49: 1973, 309-312.

196   Hamblen, Abigail Ann. "Edward Albee and the Fear of Virginia Woolf", TRACE, Lond., No. 68, 1969, 198-203.

197   Hanquart, Evelyne. "Humanisme féministe ou humanisme au féminin: Une lecture de l'oeuvre romanesque de Virginia Woolf et E. M. Forster", ÉTUDES ANGLAISES, Paris, 26: 1973, 278-289.

198   Harper, Howard M. "Mrs. Woolf and Mrs. Dalloway", THE CLASSIC BRITISH NOVEL, Athens, Georgia, 1972, 220-239.

199   Hartley, Lodwick. "Of Time and Mrs. Woolf", SEWANEE REVIEW, Sewanee, Vol. XLVII, Apr-June 1939, 235-241.

      The target of attack in this study is Woolf's characterization. Her characters are elfin spirits and fade out of the reader's mind.

200   Hartman, Geoffrey H. "Virginia's Web", CHICAGO REVIEW, XLV: 4, Spring 1961, 20-32.

201   Hashmi, Shahnaz. "Indirect Style in TO THE LIGHTHOUSE", THE INDIAN JOURNAL OF ENGLISH STUDIES, Calcutta, Vol. II, No. 1, 1961, pp. 112-120.

      Suggests that in TO THE LIGHTHOUSE Virginia Woolf rejects the conventional novelist's use of direct narrative and authorial comment, and employs certain devices such as hints, suggestions, images, and symbols which enable the reader to live in the minds of the novel's characters and to share their moods and feelings.

202   Havard-Williams, Peter and Margaret. "Mystical Experience in Virginia Woolf's THE WAVES", ESSAYS IN CRITICISM, Lond., Vol. 4, No. 1, 1954, pp. 71-84.

      A philosophical approach to Virginia Woolf's novels. Discuss THE WAVES in terms of its mystic vision.

203   _____. "Bateau Ivre: The Symbol of the Sea in Virginia Woolf's THE WAVES", ENGLISH STUDIES, Amsterdam, Vol. 34, February 1953, pp. 9-17.

      Think that Rhoda's difficulty in bringing out the vague, elusive flux of her mind has significant points of affinity with the creative artist's problem of embodying the perceptions of the unconscious mind.

204   _____. "Perceptive Contemplation in the Work of Virginia Woolf", ENGLISH STUDIES, Amsterdam, Vol. XXXV, 1954, pp. 97-116.

      Maintain that the states of mind of Virginia Woolf's

characters--"the clouded states of consciousness" in which
their minds "hover between dream and reality"--have important
parallels with the nature and process of artistic creation.

205   Heine, Elizabeth.   "The Evolution of the Interludes in THE
      WAVES", VIRGINIA WOOLF QUARTERLY, San Diego, 1:   No. 1, Fall
      1972, 60-80.

206   Henig, Suzanne.   "Virginia Woolf and Lady Murasaki", LITERATURE
      EAST AND WEST, New Paltz, New York, Vol. XI, 1967, 121-123.

      About Virginia Woolf's interest in Eastern literature and her
      appreciation of Lady Murasaki's novel TALE OF GENJI which she
      reviewed in the TIMES LITERARY SUPPLEMENT.

207   _____. "D. H. Lawrence and Virginia Woolf", THE
      D. H. LAWRENCE REVIEW, University of Arkansas, 2:   1969, 665-
      671.

      Notes the change in Virginia Woolf's attitude to Lawrence in
      the essay THE MOMENT.

208   Herrick, Robert.   "The Works of Mrs. Woolf", THE SATURDAY RE-
      VIEW OF LITERATURE, New York, December 5, 1931, p. 346.

      A characteristic attitude to Virginia Woolf in the thirties.
      Describes Mrs. Woolf's fiction as the "multiple reflection of
      a dying race".   Finds her characters fragile and anaemic hav-
      ing no "vital sense of life".

209   Higdon, David Leon.   "Mrs. Ramsay's First Name", VIRGINIA WOOLF
      QUARTERLY, San Diego, California, 1:   No. 2, Winter 1973, 46-
      47.

210   _____. "Three Studies of Virginia Woolf" (Rev. art.),
      STUDIES IN THE NOVEL (North Texas State University), 3:   1971,
      108-116.

211   Hildick, Wallace.   "In That Solitary Room", KENYON REVIEW, Ohio,
      Vol. 27, No. 2, Spring 1965, p. 312.

      Finds a Dickensian flavour in Virginia Woolf's descriptions of
      London.   Dickens became "a sort of projected presence" in the
      "fabric of her prose".

212   Himmelfark, Gertrude.   "Mr. Stephen and Mrs. Ramsay: The Vic-
      torian as Intellectual", THE TWENTIETH CENTURY, London, Vol.
      CLII, No. 910, December 1952, pp. 513-525.

      On the kinship between Mr. Ramsay (TO THE LIGHTHOUSE) and Vir-
      ginia Woolf's father Sir Leslie Stephen.   Mr. Ramsay had, as
      Stephen did, "starved himself as an intellectual ... had ema-
      ciated his sensibility, constricted his faith, stunted his
      imagination".

213   Hoare, Dorothy M. "Virginia Woolf", THE CAMBRIDGE REVIEW,
       Cambridge, October 16, 1931, pp. 27-28.

       Maintains that the chief problem of Virginia Woolf is "to make
       the moment perfect, to harmonize discords, to attain a central
       significance".

214   Hoffmann, A. C. "Subject and Object and the Nature of Reality:
       The Dialectic of TO THE LIGHTHOUSE", TEXAS STUDIES IN LITERATURE
       AND LANGUAGE, Austin, Texas, Vol. XIII, No. 4, Winter 1972,
       691-703.

       "... Virginia Woolf's vision of reality is a subject-object re-
       lationship in which there is an organic interaction between hu-
       man consciousness and the object being perceived...."

215   Hoffman, Charles C. "TO THE LIGHTHOUSE", THE EXPLICATOR, Vir-
       ginia, November 1951, item 13.

       The lighthouse, the bowl of fruit and Lily's final stroke of
       the brush constitute integral parts of the theme and structure
       of TO THE LIGHTHOUSE.

216   _____. "Virginia Woolf's Manuscript Revisions of
       THE YEARS", PMLA, New York, Vol. 84, No. 1, January 1969, pp.
       79-89.

       Shows how in revising the manuscript of THE YEARS Virginia
       Woolf dropped the expository essays on social questions in the
       earlier portions of her original manuscript and came to depend
       on the characters' inner vision. Considers it a defect of the
       novel because "this attempt to modify the form of the tradi-
       tional family chronicle by bridging the years through moments
       of vision fails because there is a lack of balance between fact
       and vision".

217   _____. "From Short Story to Novel: The Manuscript
       Revisions of Virginia Woolf's MRS. DALLOWAY", MODERN FICTION
       STUDIES, Lafayette, Indiana, Vol. XIV, Summer 1966, pp. 171-
       186.

       "The revisions show how the thematic focus was shifted from the
       external political and social conflict to the internal con-
       flict...."

218   _____. "Fact and Fantasy in ORLANDO: Virginia
       Woolf's Manuscript Revisions", TEXAS STUDIES IN LITERATURE AND
       LANGUAGE, Austin, Texas, Vol. 10, 1968, pp. 435-444.

       Shows the changes such as chapter divisions and dates in the
       published version of ORLANDO.

219   _____. "From Lunch to Dinner: Virginia Woolf's Ap-
       prenticeship", TEXAS STUDIES IN LITERATURE AND LANGUAGE,

Austin, Texas, 10: 4, Wint. 1969, 609-627.

Argues that the manuscript versions of THE VOYAGE OUT and
NIGHT AND DAY show that Virginia Woolf's shift from the traditional narrative technique to the experiments in her later
novels was not sudden. The first two novels "reveal the seed
of Virginia Woolf's dissatisfaction with the realist's approach and her attempt to break out of that mould".

220 _____. "The 'Real' Mrs. Dalloway", THE UNIVERSITY
OF KANSAS CITY REVIEW, Kansas City, Missouri, Vol. 22, Spring
1956, pp. 204-208.

The "real" Mrs. Dalloway is a "complex personality" who lives
as much in the "experiences and memories" of others as in those
of her own.

221 Hogan, J. P. "Virginia Woolf", THE ADELPHI, Lond., July-
September 1945, 191-192.

A sharp reaction against Virginia Woolf's aestheticism and her
Bloomsbury values: "Her exquisite sensibility did, in the
microcosm, epitomize the malaise of a rotten society".

222 Hollingsworth, Keith. "Freud and the Riddle of MRS. DALLOWAY",
STUDIES IN HONOUR OF JOHN WILCOX BY MEMBERS OF THE ENGLISH DE-
PARTMENT, Wayne State University, Detroit, ed. A. D. Wallace
and W. O. Ross, 1958, 239-249.

Examines, in depth, the psychological element in MRS. DALLOWAY.
Interprets Septimus's death-instinct in Freudian terms.

223 Holms, J. F. "MRS. DALLOWAY" (Rev. art.), THE CALENDAR OF
MODERN LETTERS, LOND., 1, V, July 1925, 404-405.

The article looked ahead to the SCRUTINY line of attack on
Virginia Woolf's work /See No. 258/. Condemns Mrs. Woolf's
impressionistic style, and maintains that "her writing conveys
an effect of automatism that is curious and aesthetically cor-
rupt". Complains that Woolf's "treatment of character and human relations is almost entirely devoid of psychological and
aesthetic truth".

224 Howarth, R. G. "Day Spring of Virginia Woolf", SOUTHERLY,
Sidney, 3: April 1942, 18-21.

Argues that the conventional craft of NIGHT AND DAY and its
topical allusions indicate that the book was written before
THE VOYAGE OUT, although it came out later probably because it
was originally rejected by the publishers.

225 Hulcopp, John F. "Virginia Woolf's Diaries: Some Reflections
After Reading Them and a Censure of Mr. Holroyd", BULLETIN OF
THE NEW YORK PUBLIC LIBRARY, New York, 75: 1971, 301-310.

Maintains that Virginia Woolf's diaries do not support the conventional view that she was a "sexless, aetherial creature who drifted mistily through dream-like days unconcerned with practical affairs, social issues, moral problems".

226   Hungerford, E. A. "My Tunnelling Process: The Method of MRS. DALLOWAY", MODERN FICTION STUDIES, Lafayette, 3: 2, Summer 1956, 164-167.

       A detailed analysis of the stream of consciousness technique in MRS. DALLOWAY.

227   _____. "Mrs. Woolf, Freud, and J. D. Beresford", LITERATURE AND PSYCHOLOGY, New York, 5: 3, August 1955, 49-51.

       Thinks that Woolf's review of J. D. Beresford's novel AN IMPERFECT MOTHER in the TIMES LITERARY SUPPLEMENT shows that even five years before the appearance of MRS. DALLOWAY, she "knew enough about the Freudian style of the interpretation of dreams".

228   Hunting, Constance. "The Technique of Persuasion in ORLANDO", MODERN FICTION STUDIES, Lafayette, ii: 1, February 1956, 17-23.

       Examines the various devices used by Woolf in ORLANDO to persuade the reader of the new concepts of time and sex.

229   Hynes, Samuel. "The Whole Contention Between Mr. Bennett and Mrs. Woolf", NOVEL: A FORUM ON FICTION, Brown University, 1: 10, 1967, 34-44.

       Discusses the significance in the history of the English novel of the Woolf-Bennett conflict over the modes of fiction.

230   Izzo, C. "Testimonianze sul Bloomsbury Group", STUDI IN ONORE DI VITTORIO LUGLI E DIEGO VALERI, Venice, 1962.

231   Jackson, David. "Virginia Woolf: The Portrait of a Lady", MUSEUM NOTES, Rhode Island School of Design, Providence, Fall 1954, 9-12.

       Mainly biographical.

232   Jackson, Gertrude. "Virginia Woolf's A HAUNTED HOUSE: Reality and 'Moment of Being' in Her KEW GARDENS", in Bauer, G. F. K. Stanzel and F. Zaic (eds.), FESTSCHRIFT PROF. DR. HERBERT KOZIOL ZUM SIEBZIGSTEN GEBURTSTAG (Wiener Beitrage Zur englisch-en Philologie 75), Vienna, 1973.

233   Jones, E. B. C. "Virginia Woolf and E. M. Forster", THE ENGLISH NOVELISTS, ed. Derek Verschoyle, Lond., 1936, pp. 261-263.

Describes Virginia Woolf's literary characteristics and her development as a novelist.

234   Josephson, Matthew. "Virginia Woolf and the Modern Novel" (Rev. art.), THE NEW REPUBLIC, New York, Vol. LXVI, April 15, 1931, pp. 239-241.

A general survey of Virginia Woolf's novels up to ORLANDO. Maintains that her contribution to the modern novel lay in her "remarkable extension of the zone of sensibility".

235   Kaehele, Sharon and Howard German. "TO THE LIGHTHOUSE: Symbol and Vision", BUCKNELL REVIEW, Lewisburg, Pennsylvania, Vol. X, No. 4, May 1962, 328-346.

The critics discuss how the various themes of the novel are unified through the symbol of the lighthouse and Lily's vision.

236   Kelsey, Electra Mary. "Virginia Woolf and the She-condition", SEWANEE REVIEW, Sewanee, Vol. XXXIX, October-December 1931, 425-444.

Deals at length with the concept of the androgynous mind in Woolf's fiction. Shows how in Mrs. Woolf's novels the masculine and feminine principles work together. She thinks as a 'man' but she feels as a 'woman'. The feminine aspects of life such as emotion and sensibility motivate her creative work while masculine traits like logic and analysis characterize her critical writings.

237   King, Merton P. "THE WAVES and the Androgynous Mind", UNIVERSITY REVIEW, Kansas City, XXX: 2, December 1963, 128-134.

Discusses how the characters of THE WAVES represent the concept of the androgynous mind as a "theory of writing" and as a "philosophy of life". Bernard is the alter ego of Mrs. Woolf.

238   Koeztur, G. "Virginia Woolf and the Dilemma of the Modern English Novel", ANNALES UNIVERSITATIS SCIENTIARUM BUDAPESTIENSIS DE ROLANDO EOTUOS NOMINATAE, Sectio Philologica, Tomux IV, 1963, 139-54.

239   Kondo, Ineko. "Virginia Woolf to E. M. Forster", EIGO SEINER /The Rising Generation/, Tokyo, 116: 1970, 61-66 /In Japanese/.

240   Kreutz, Irving. "Mr. Bennett and Mrs. Woolf", MODERN FICTION STUDIES, Lafayette, VIII: 2, Summer 1962, 103-115.

Questions Virginia Woolf's judgement of Arnold Bennett. Finds in HILDA LESSWAYS Bennett's interest in the analysis of human personality.

241   Kronenberger, Louis. "Virginia Woolf as Critic" (Rev. art.),
       THE NATION, New York, 155: 16, Oct. 17, 1942, 382-385. Re-
       printed in his THE REPUBLIC OF LETTERS: ESSAYS ON VARIOUS
       WRITERS, New York, 1955, 244-249.

       Thinks that Virginia Woolf's strength as a critic did not lie
       in any systematic principles of criticism: "She will survive
       not as a critic, but as a literary essayist recording the ad-
       ventures of a soul among congenial masterpieces".

242   Kumar, Shiv K. "Memory in Virginia Woolf and Bergson", THE
       UNIVERSITY OF KANSAS CITY REVIEW, Kansas City, XXVI, 3, March
       1960, 235-239.

       Maintains that like Bergson Virginia Woolf believed that mem-
       ory acts by the law of association and that past experiences
       could be revived in their totality.

243   _____. "A Positive Note on Bergson and Virginia
       Woolf", THE LITERARY CRITERION, Mysore, India, Vol. IV, No.
       4, Summer 1961, 27-31.

       Unlike John Graham ("Negative Note on Bergson and Virginia
       Woolf", ESSAYS IN CRITICISM, January 1956), Kumar feels that
       "in her deepest convictions Virginia Woolf was a Bergsonian".
       Shows the resemblance between Virginia Woolf's view of real-
       ity and Bergson's--"her concept of duration and the Bergson-
       ian flux".

244   Laing, D. A. "An Addendum to the Virginia Woolf Bibliography",
       NOTES AND QUERIES, Lond., Vol. 19, No. 9, September 1972, p.
       338.

       Thinks that Virginia Woolf's foreword to the catalogue of
       paintings by Vanessa Bell contains some of her /Mrs. Woolf's7
       "basic thoughts about art", the chief of which is her empha-
       sis on the personal vision of reality.

245   Lakshmi, Vijay. "Crystallizing the Amorphous: Virginia
       Woolf's Theory of the Creative Process", THE INDIAN JOURNAL
       OF ENGLISH STUDIES, Calcutta, Vol. XIII, 1972, 114-121.

       Virginia Woolf "shapes the iridescent and the amorphous sub-
       stance of life into a work of art".

246   _____. "Virginia Woolf and E. M. Forster: A Study
       in Inter Criticism", BANASTHALI PATRIKA, Rajasthan, India, 16:
       1971, 8-18.

       "Forster could reject criticism as a mere secondary activity
       but Virginia Woolf could not. Neither can Forster keep up
       the detached outlook of an objective observer nor can he be-
       come the writer's accomplice. Virginia Woolf focuses her
       perspective as it were with that of the writer and then starts
       discovering the works".

247 _____. "The Unviewed Room: An Interpretation of the Room Analogy in Virginia Woolf's Critical Writings", RAJASTHAN UNIVERSITY STUDIES IN ENGLISH, Jaipur, India, Vol. VI, 1972, 64-69.

"Virginia Woolf uses the room analogy to symbolize the mind. She likes adventuring into different minds. A mind is like a new room to her ... The room presents the inner workings of the mind ... It is the recipient of impressions from the external world. The room is the creative mind".

248 _____. "Virginia Woolf: The Self Behind the Many-Faced Mask" (Rev. art.), THE RAJASTHAN UNIVERSITY STUDIES IN ENGLISH, Jaipur, India, Vol. VII, 1974, 86-91.

Reviews RECOLLECTIONS OF VIRGINIA WOOLF by Joan Russell Noble and VIRGINIA WOOLF: A BIOGRAPHY by Quentin Bell. Feels that both these books fail to explore the total personality of Virginia Woolf.

249 _____. "The Solid and the Intangible: Virginia Woolf's Theory of the Androgynous Mind", THE LITERARY CRITERION, Mysore, India, Vol. X, No. 1, Winter 1971, 28-34.

Sees a close link between Virginia Woolf's view of the androgynous mind and her theory of fiction: Virginia Woolf believes in the combination of dissimilar elements, the material and the spiritual, the outer and the inner. "The novelist, while he receives impressions as they fall upon the mind, has to be impersonal. He has to be immersed in life and not to be away from it forgetting his own personality".

250 Lalou, René. "Le Sentiment de l'unité humaine chez Virginia Woolf et Aldous Huxley", EUROPE, Paris, October 15, 1937, 266-272.

251 Lanoire, M. "Le témoignage de MRS. DALLOWAY", LES LETTRES, Paris, 17: 1930.

252 Latham, Jacqueline. "The Origin of MRS. DALLOWAY", NOTES AND QUERIES, Lond., Vol. 13, No. 3, March 1966, 98-99.

Traces the origin of MRS. DALLOWAY to Virginia Woolf's earlier short story MRS. DALLOWAY IN BOND STREET. This is evident from the opening passages of the novel.

253 _____. "The Model for Clarissa Dalloway--Kitty Maxse", NOTES AND QUERIES, Lond., Vol. 16, July 1969, 262-63.

Disagrees with Jean Guiguet's opinion (VIRGINIA WOOLF AND HER WORKS, p. 228) that Clarissa Dalloway was based on Lady Ottoline Morrell. Argues with corroborative evidence that Katherine Maxse, the society lady who was known to the Stephen family, was actually the model for Clarissa Dalloway.

254 _____. "Archetypal Figures in MRS. DALLOWAY",
NEUPHILOLOGISCHE MITTEILUNGEN, Helsinki, 71: 1970, 480-488.

255 _____. "The Manuscript Revisions of Virginia
Woolf's MRS. DALLOWAY: A Postscript", MODERN FICTION STUDIES,
Lafayette, Indiana, 18: Autumn 1972, 475-476.

Questions the accuracy of Prof. Hartman's opinion about the
MS of MRS. DALLOWAY and gives alternate readings of the MS.
Thinks that the MS suggests a correspondence between Septimus
and Virginia Woolf.

256 Lavin, J. A. "The First Editions of Virginia Woolf's TO THE
LIGHTHOUSE", PROOF: YEARBOOK OF AMERICAN BIBLIOGRAPHICAL
AND TEXTUAL STUDIES, Michigan, 2: 1972, 185-211.

257 Leaska, Mitchell A. "Virginia Woolf's THE VOYAGE OUT: Character Deduction and the Function of Ambiguity", VIRGINIA
WOOLF QUARTERLY, San Diego, 1, No. 2, Winter 1973, 18-41.

258 Leavis, F. R. "After TO THE LIGHTHOUSE" (Rev. art.), SCRUTINY,
Cambridge, X, 3, January 1942, 295-298.

A classic in Woolf criticism. Dr. Leavis questions the whole
basis of Virginia Woolf's aesthetic theory. His central
thesis is summed up in the statement about Woolf: "A sensitive mind whose main interests are not endorsed by the pre-
dominant interests of the world it lives in, and whose talent
and professional skill seem to have no real public importance".

259 Lehmann, John. "Virginia Woolf", WRITERS OF TODAY, Lond.,
Vol. 2, ed. Denys Val Baker, 1948, pp. 73-84.

Maintains that Virginia Woolf "enlarged the sensibility of
her time and changed English literature". Through her 'mem-
orable' symbols she expressed what few modern writers have
done: the mystery of life and death and love, the beauty of
life as well as its terror and anguish.

260 _____. "Virginia Woolf", FOLIOS OF NEW WRITINGS,
Lond., Spring 1941, pp. 44-46.

Although Virginia Woolf was a "socialist" and had sympathy
for the working classes, she could not, she felt, identify
herself with the poor because of her upper-middle-class
origin. All she could do was to remain a "sympathetic observer". This attitude was sincere and honest.

261 Lemonnier, L. "Le dernier roman: THE YEARS", IMPRESSIONS,
Paris, 5: 1938 (Sp. No. on Virginia Woolf).

262 Lewis, A. J. "From THE HOURS to MRS. DALLOWAY", THE BRITISH
MUSEUM QUARTERLY, Lond., XX, No. VIII, 1964, 15-17.

Examines the various stages in the composition of MRS. DAL-
LOWAY to show that Virginia Woolf broke free from her earlier vague airy lyricism and combined it with a "tougher
element".

263 Leyburn, Ellen Douglas. "Virginia Woolf's Judgement of Henry
     James", MODERN FICTION STUDIES, Lafayette, Indiana, Vol. 5,
     Summer 1959, 166-169.

     Suggests that Virginia Woolf did not have much to learn from
     Henry James. Her genius was essentially lyrical while that
     of James was dramatic.

264 Liberto, Sarah. "The 'Perpetual Pageant' of Art and Life in
     TO THE LIGHTHOUSE", DESCANT, Fort Worth, Texas, IX, Winter
     1965, 35-43.

     "The happiness that Mrs. Woolf knew is the joy of creation,
     the sense of fulfillment that the artist experiences in
     those occasional fleeting moments of being in which art and
     life, form and flux, appearance and reality, merge".

265 Little, Judith. "Heroism in TO THE LIGHTHOUSE", IMAGES OF
     WOMEN IN FICTION: FEMINIST PERSPECTIVES, Bowling Green,
     Ohio, 1972, 237-242.

266 Lombardo, A. "Il diario di Virginia Woolf", CONVIVIUM,
     Bologna, Italy, 23: 1955.

267 Lorberg, Aileen D. "Virginia Woolf: Benevolent Satirist",
     THE PERSONALIST, California, Vol. XXXIII, No. 1, Winter 1952,
     148-158.

     Deals with the humorous aspect of Virginia Woolf's writing
     which has not received enough critical attention. She was a
     humorist but her satire was not prompted by any serious cor-
     rective purpose. Discusses A ROOM OF ONE'S OWN, MR. BENNETT
     AND MRS BROWN, FLUSH and MRS. DALLOWAY.

268 Lund, Mary Graham. "The Androgynous Mind: Woolf and Eliot",
     RENASCENCE, Wisconsin, Vol. XII, No. 2, Winter 1960, 74-78.

     Discusses the problem of alienation in Virginia Woolf and
     T. S. Eliot, and their quest for integration. Examines THE
     WAVES and THE COCKTAIL PARTY from this angle.

269 MacCarthy, Desmond. "Phantasmagoria" (Rev. art.), THE SUN-
     DAY TIMES, Lond., October 14, 1928.

     An impartial assessment of Virginia Woolf's weakness and
     strength as a novelist by one of her Bloomsbury friends.
     Finds her achievement in the depiction of private thoughts
     and dreams and her failure in the creation of "memorable
     individual characters".

270   Majumdar, R.   "Virginia Woolf and Thoreau", THOREAU SOCIETY
      BULLETIN, New York, Fall 1969.

      Notes the affinity between the two writers in their attitude
      to reality and their preoccupation with the problem of human
      relations.

271   Mansfield, Katherine.   "A Ship Comes into the Harbour", NOVELS
      AND NOVELISTS, Lond., 1930, 107-111.

      Praises, with reservations, Virginia Woolf's NIGHT AND DAY.
      Focuses on the affinity between Jane Austen and Virginia Woolf.
      Thinks that Woolf's characters unlike Austen's are "lifeless".

272   Manuel, M.   "Virginia Woolf as the Common Reader", THE LITER-
      ARY CRITERION, Mysore, India, Vol. VII, No. 2, Summer 1966, pp.
      28-32.

      Emphasises the close relation between Virginia Woolf's critical
      essays and her novels.   "Her collected criticism is the work-
      shop criticism of a novelist rather than the objective evalua-
      tion of writers and their works".

273   Marcel, Gabriel.   "LES VAGUES, par Virginia Woolf", LA NOUVELLE
      REVUE FRANÇAISE, Paris, Vol. XXXVIII, No. 224, February 1932,
      303-308.

      Largely unfavourable.   Attacks Virginia Woolf's subjective
      technique in which he finds "something arbitrary, an absence
      of inner necessity".

274   Marder, Herbert.   "Beyond the Lighthouse: THE YEARS", BUCKNELL
      REVIEW, Lewisburg, Pennsylvania, Vol. XV, No. 1, March 1967,
      pp. 61-70.

      Argues that THE YEARS is not a return to the conventional
      novel as some critics think it is.   It is very much character-
      istic of Virginia Woolf and shows the same "conflict between
      the inner life and outer forms of conventions" as do her ear-
      lier novels.   But unlike them THE YEARS succeeds in bringing
      into harmony the inner and the outer, "the life of solitude"
      and "the life of society", fact and vision.   The novel's char-
      acters and symbols help to create this impression.

275   _____.   "Virginia Woolf's 'System that did not Shut
      Out'", PAPERS ON LANGUAGE AND LITERATURE, Southern Illinois
      University, Edwardsville, Illinois, V,   10, Winter 1969, 106-
      111.

276   Masui, J.   "Virginia Woolf", LE FLAMBEAU, Brussels, 15:   1932.

277   Maurois, André.   "Première rencontre avec Virginia Woolf", LES
      NOUVELLES LITTERAIRES, Paris, August 13, 1927, p. 1.

278   May, Keith M.   "The Symbol of Painting in Virginia Woolf's TO

THE LIGHTHOUSE", A REVIEW OF ENGLISH LITERATURE, Lond., VIII, No. 2, April 1967, 91-98.

Thinks that Lily Briscoe and Virginia Woolf have a common aim. Lily seeks to organize different colours and masses into a significant design and Mrs. Woolf's purpose, like Lily's, is to create harmony and order out of the flux of experience.

279   Mayoux, Jean-Jacques. "Le Roman de l'Espace et du Temps: Virginia Woolf", REVUE ANGLO-AMÉRICAINE, Paris, 7, April 1930, 312-326.

280   _____. "A Propos d'ORLANDO de Virginia Woolf", EUROPE, Paris, Vol. 22, January 15, 1930, 117-122.

281   _____. "Sur un livre de Virginia Woolf", REVUE ANGLO-AMÉRICAINE, Paris, Vol. 5, June 1928, 424-438.

282   McConnel, Frank D. "Death Among the Apple Trees: THE WAVES and the World of Things", BUCKNELL REVIEW, Pennsylvania, Vol. XVI, No. 3, December 1968, 22-39.

Argues that in THE WAVES Virginia Woolf seeks a synthesis of the subjective and the objective, the aesthetic and the phenomenal.

283   Mc Gehee, Edward Glenn. "Virginia Woolf: Experimentalist Within Tradition", BULLETIN OF VANDERBILT UNIVERSITY: ABSTRACT OF THESIS, Vanderbilt, Vol. XLIII, No. 11, August 1942, p. 40.

Thinks that Virginia Woolf did not break away from her immediate predecessors: "Writers like Peacock, Sterne, and Hardy were her real teachers".

284   Mc Intyre, Clara F. "Is Virginia Woolf a Feminist?" THE PERSONALIST, Los Angeles, Vol. XLI, No. 2, April 1960, 176-184.

Thinks that "it is probable that Virginia Woolf's feeling about men and women developed from her relation with her father".

285   Meijer Greiner, Mechtilt. "Boeken over Virginia Woolf", KUNST EN CULTUUR, Brussels, 29 Nov: 24-25, 1973.

286   Mellers, W. H. "Mrs. Woolf and Life" (Rev. art.), SCRUTINY, Cambridge, June 1937, 71-75. Reprinted in Eric Bentley (ed.), THE IMPORTANCE OF SCRUTINY, New York, 1948, 376-827.

Another typical example of the SCRUTINY case against Virginia Woolf. Two major objections to Mrs. Woolf's work are: that she is not a novelist but a sensuous impressionist and that she lacks a clear and co-ordinated attitude to life.

287   _____. "Virginia Woolf: The Last Phase", KENYON REVIEW, Ohio, Vol. IV, Winter 1942, 381-87.

Much the same line of attack as in his earlier article. Asserts that BETWEEN THE ACTS also shows faults similar to those of Woolf's previous books.

288   Mendez, Charlotte Walker. "I Need a Little Language", VIRGINIA WOOLF QUARTERLY, San Diego, 1,1, Fall 1972, 87-105.

289   Miller, David N. "Authorial Point of View in Virginia Woolf's MRS. DALLOWAY", JOURNAL OF NARRATIVE TECHNIQUE (Dept. of English, Eastern Michigan University), Vol. 2, No. 2, May 1972, 125-132.

Suggests that in MRS. DALLOWAY Woolf has "provided the impression of narration through multiple, fallible consciousness while retaining the privilege of direct communication with the readers". Examines the various devices used by Woolf to communicate the authorial point of view.

290   Miller, J. Hillis. "Virginia Woolf's All Soul's Day: The Omniscient Narrator in MRS. DALLOWAY", THE SHAKEN REALIST: ESSAYS IN MODERN LITERATURE IN HONOUR OF FREDERICK J. HOFFMAN. ed. Melvin J. Miller and John B. Vickery, Baton Rouge, Louisiana, 1970.

291   Miller, W. J. and Dinnerstein, D. "Woolf's ORLANDO", EXPLICATOR, Virginia, Vol. XIX, No. 6, March 1961, Item 6.

To show "how to accept and help perpetuate an artistic tradition largely masculine in nature without becoming masculine herself" ... is Woolf's 'triumph' in ORLANDO.

292   Mitchison, Naomi. "Two Moderns: Virginia Woolf and T. S. Eliot", THE WEEKEND REVIEW, Lond., October 15, 1932, p. 447.

Thinks that like T. S. Eliot Virginia Woolf is also acutely aware of the modern problem of alienation. She is not an individualist.

293   Mollach, Francis L. "Thematic and Structural Unity in MRS. DALLOWAY", THOTH (Dept. of English, Syracuse University), V: 2, Spring 1964, 62-73.

294   Moloney, Michael F. "The Enigma of Time: Proust, Virginia Woolf and Faulkner", THOUGHT, New York, Vol. 37, 1957, 69-85.

The concept of fluid time in Virginia Woolf's novels is discussed at length.

295   Monroe, Elizabeth N. "The Inception of Mrs. Woolf's Art", COLLEGE ENGLISH, Illinois, Vol. 2, No. 3, December 1940, 217-230.

A characteristic sample of the anti-aesthetic reaction against Virginia Woolf's novels: "Mrs. Woolf's art reduces social consciousness almost to its lowest level..."

296   _____. "Virginia Woolf", THE NOVEL AND SOCIETY:
A CRITICAL STUDY OF THE MODERN NOVEL, Chapel Hill, North
Carolina, 1941, 188-224.

Admires Virginia Woolf's insight into subtle moods but criticizes her "movement away from reality and from a compact society towards aestheticism".

297   Moody, A. D. "The Unmasking of Clarissa Dalloway", A REVIEW
OF ENGLISH LITERATURE, Lond., Vol. 3, No. 1, January 1962,
67-79.

Argues that what Virginia Woolf wanted to criticize in MRS.
DALLOWAY is the society of Clarissa Dalloway but she did not
succeed, and "the imperfections in this criticism are to be
attributed to her having attempted something beyond her
grasp". Her talent did not reach to an adequate rendering of
the novel's concerns.

298   Morgenstern, Barry. "The Self-Conscious Narrator in JACOB'S
ROOM", MODERN FICTION STUDIES, Lafayette, Indiana, 18: Autumn 1972, 351-361.

Thinks that Joan Bennett and R. L. Chambers have missed one
major focus of Woolf's novels: their narrators and narrative
commentary. Virginia Woolf did not eliminate the narrator
from JACOB'S ROOM. Mrs. Flanders is the self-conscious narrator.

299   Morra, U. "Il nuova romanzo Inglese: Virginia Woolf", LA
CULTURA, Rome, January 1931.

300   Mortimer, Raymond. "Mrs. Woolf and Mr. Strachey", THE BOOK-
MAN, New York, LXVIII, February 1929, 625-629.

A general consideration of Virginia Woolf's work up to OR-
LANDO. Mainly sympathetic.

301   _____. "Virginia Woolf", CHANNEL PACKET, Lond.,
1942, 27-32.

Admires Mrs. Woolf's 'fine' perception, but finds her characterization 'fugitive' and 'wraith-like' and her construction
'weak'.

302   Muir, Edwin. "Virginia Woolf", THE NATION, New York, Vol.
122, No. 3182, June 30, 1926, 721-723.

Provides a new attitude to Mrs. Woolf's characterization.
Considers her approach to characterization truer than the
external approach, because it enabled her to understand her
characters' reactions to each other "more naturally".

303   _____. "Virginia Woolf", THE BOOKMAN, New York ,

Vol. 74, December 1931, p. 367.

Gives high praise to THE WAVES. Thinks that in this novel Woolf is dealing directly with "immediate and essential truths of experience" and the result is "an authentic and unique masterpiece".

304   Muller, Herbert. "Virginia Woolf and Feminine Fiction", THE SATURDAY REVIEW OF LITERATURE, New York, 15: February 6, 1937, 3-4 and 14-16. Reprinted in his MODERN FICTION: A STUDY OF VALUES, New York, 1937.

Complains about Virginia Woolf's "over-refinement". Argues that although in expressing minute and subtle nuances of her characters Mrs. Woolf is unparalleled in English fiction, she is nevertheless much too refined and rarefied to come to grips with concrete situations, and her characters are 'fragile' and 'anaemic'. This position is taken further in Robert Herrick's article (See No. 208).

305   Naremore, James. "A World Without a Self: The Novels of Virginia Woolf", A FORUM ON FICTION, Brown University, Rhode Island, 5,2, Winter 1972, 122-134.

"Virginia Woolf takes us to the point where the personality itself becomes dissolved in communion with what is outside ... and beyond".

306   _____. "The 'Orts and Fragments' in BETWEEN THE ACTS", BALL STATE UNIVERSITY FORUM, Muncie, Indiana, 14, 1, 1973, 59-69.

307   Nathan, M. "'Visualisation' et Vision chez Virginia Woolf", REVUE DES LETTRES MODERNES, Paris, 5: 1957-1958.

308   Neuschäffer, Walter. "Virginia Woolf", DOSTOJEWSKIJ'S EINFLUSS AUF DEM ENGLISCHEN ROMAN, Heidelberg, 1935, 81-88.

Discusses Dostoevsky's influence on Virginia Woolf. Shows the similarity between Woolf's conception of human personality and that of Dostoevsky. Also refers to the sense of enigma and mystery in the two writers.

309   Nicolson, Harold. "The Writing of Virginia Woolf", THE LISTENER, Lond., November 18, 1931, p. 64.

Stresses the poetic style of Woolf's novels. Thinks that Virginia Woolf is more a lyric poet than a novelist. She adds, with the help of her lyrical style, "whole tracts of her new territory to our experience".

310   Noel, Roger. "Nathalie Sarraute's Criticism of Virginia Woolf", REVUE DES LANGUES VIVANTES, Brussels, 36, 1970, 266-271.

311 O'Faolain, Sean. "Narcissa and Lucifer: An Essay on Vir-
     ginia Woolf and James Joyce", NEW WORLD WRITING, New York,
     Vol. 10, November 1956, 161-175.

     A severe attack on Virginia Woolf's subjective approach to
     the novel. Complains that unlike Joyce "she was too absorbed
     in her own private self ever to wed experience fully".

312 Osawa, M. "Virginia Woolf and Pater", NEW ENGLISH AND AMERI-
     CAN LITERATURE, No. 1, 1948.

313 Overcarsh, F. L. "The Lighthouse, Face to Face",ACCENT, Il-
     linois, X, Winter 1950, 107.

314 Ozick, Cynthia. "Mrs. Virginia Woolf", COMMENTARY, New York,
     56, ii, 1973, 33-44.

315 Pachmuss, T. "Dostoevsky, Werfel, and Virginia Woolf: In-
     fluences and Confluences", COMPARATIVE LITERATURE STUDIES,
     University of Illinois, IX, No. 4, December 1972, 416-428.

     The Woolf-Dostoevsky relationship is highlighted. Dostoevsky's
     profound psychological analysis, his emphasis on inner life,
     the agony of loneliness and the mystery of death deeply im-
     pressed Virginia Woolf.

316 Page, Alex. "A Dangerous Day: Mrs. Dalloway Discovers Her
     Double", MODERN FICTION STUDIES, Vol. VII, No. 2, Summer 1961,
     115-124.

     Discusses, from the psychological point of view, the relation-
     ship between Clarissa Dalloway and Septimus Warren Smith.
     Finds important parallels between the two in their reactions
     to the world around them. Septimus is the 'id' to Clarissa's
     'ego' and the two eventually "emerge into one personality".

317 Painter, George. "Proust and Virginia Woolf", ADAM INTERNA-
     TIONAL REVIEW, Lond., Vol. 37, 1972, 17-23.

     Finds in Proust and Woolf a common quest for reality.

318 Parsons, T. "Virginia Woolf's Last Letters", TIMES LITERARY
     SUPPLEMENT, Lond., July 13, 1973, 808.

     About the three letters Virginia Woolf wrote on the last morn-
     ing of her life: two to her husband and one to her sister.
     One of the letters to Leonard Woolf together with his comments
     is reproduced.

319 Payne, Michael. "The Eclipse of Order: The Ironic Structure
     of THE WAVES", MODERN FICTION STUDIES, Vol. XV, No. 2, Summer
     1969, pp. 209-218.

     Suggests that "the central theme /In THE WAVES7 is the mind's attempt to make some intelligible order and impression" and "this search for an order in existence is manifest as an existential, a psychological and an artistic quest".

320   Pedersen, Glenn. "Vision in TO THE LIGHTHOUSE", PMLA, New York, 73: December 1958, pp. 585-600.

Discusses the significance of Lily Briscoe's vision in TO THE LIGHTHOUSE. Examines the complex pattern of relationships between the novel's characters--their conflicts and final resolution in the form of Lily's vision.

321   Peel, Robert. "Virginia Woolf", THE CRITERION, Lond., Vol. XIII, No. 50, October 1933, pp. 78-96.

Stresses Woolf's intentions as a novelist. Thinks that her novels are the novels of "sensibility" where "the great human problem is the communication of personality with personality".

322   Penner, Catherine S. "The Sacred Will in MRS. DALLOWAY", THOTH, New York, 12, 11, 1972, 3-20.

323   Phelps, Gilbert H. "Virginia Woolf and the Russians", THE CAMBRIDGE REVIEW, Cambridge, October 17, 1942, 21-22.

Maintains that Russian fiction was "a primary influence" on Virginia Woolf. Notes the influence of Chekov, Tolstoy and Dostoevsky.

324   Philipson, Morris. "MRS. DALLOWAY, What's the Sense of Your Parties?" CRITICAL INQUIRY, Chicago, Vol. 1, No.1, September 1974.

325   Pimienta, L. "Virginia Woolf et ses Compagnes", IMPRESSIONS, Paris, 5: 1935 /On Virginia Woolf, Katherine Mansfield, Rosamond Lehmann and May Sinclair/.

326   Plomer, William. "A Note on Virginia Woolf", MEANJIN, Melbourne, Vol. 6, No. 1, Autumn 1947, 16-19.

Mainly biographical. Asserts that Virginia Woolf was "not in the least aloof from her own time.... She not only enjoyed meeting people but was insatiably curious about them".

327   Pratt, Annis. "Sexual Imagery in TO THE LIGHTHOUSE: A New Feminist Approach", MODERN FICTION STUDIES, Lafayette, Indiana, Vol. 18, Autumn 1972, 417-431.

"It is appropriate to describe the creative organ of Mrs. Ramsay as phallic, an internal animus or mana power which she integrates with her encircling organic, feminine powers to compensate for her husband's lack of phallic attributes. Virginia Woolf uses concrete images to express her concept of the integrated psyche "having intercourse with the man in her".

328 Proudfit, Sharon Wood. "Lily Briscoe's Painting: A Key to Personal Relationships in TO THE LIGHTHOUSE", CRITICISM, Detroit, Vol. XIII, No. 1, Winter 1971, 26-38.

Examines the nature of the relationship between Lily and Mrs. Ramsay. Lily, although she admires Mrs. Ramsay, 'the loveliest of people', yet thinks that she is wilful, commanding and has a certain 'high-handedness' about her. "Yet Lily is attracted to Mrs. Ramsay physically and desires a more permanent union with her".

329 Rachman, Shalom. "Clarissa's Attic: Virginia Woolf's MRS. DALLOWAY Reconsidered", TWENTIETH CENTURY LITERATURE, Denver, Colorado, 18, 1, January 1972, 3-18.

330 Rahv, Philip. "Mrs. Brown and Mrs. Woolf", KENYON REVIEW, Ohio, Vol. 5, Winter 1943, pp. 147-150. Reprinted in his IMAGE AND IDEA, Norfolk, New Directions, 139-143, 1957, pp. 167-171.

A piece of hostile criticism directed against Mrs. Woolf's theory of fiction. Argues that Mrs. Brown is nothing but the "product of the traditional realism of the English novel". Although Mrs. Woolf attacked Bennett, Wells and Galsworthy, she "tacitly accepted their innermost vision of reality. Hence all she could do is to turn their vices inside out--since they had 'materialized' the novel, she devoted herself to 'spiritualizing' it. Forgotten was the pledge 'never, never to desert Mrs. Brown'."

331 Ramsay, Warren. "The Claims of Language: Virginia Woolf as Symbolist", THE ENGLISH FICTION IN TRANSITION, Lafayette, Indiana, Vol. 4, No. 1, 1961, pp. 12-16.

Thinks that Woolf's use of language is similar to that of the symbolists.

332 Rantavaara, Irma. "Virginia Woolf's THE WAVES", SOCIETAS SCIENTIARUM FENNICA, Helsinki, XXVI, No. 2, 1960.

333 _____. "Ing-forms in the service of rhythm and style in Virginia Woolf's THE WAVES", NEUPHILOLOGISCHE MITTEILUNGEN, Helsinki, Vol. LXI, No. 4, 1959, 79-97.

334 Redman, Ben Ray. "The Multiple Mrs. Woolf", NEW YORK HERALD TRIBUNE, June 28, 1931, 1-6.

Describes Virginia Woolf's various experiments with fiction.

335 Richardson, Robert O. "Point of View in Virginia Woolf's THE WAVES", TEXAS STUDIES IN LANGUAGE AND LITERATURE, Austin, Texas, 14: Winter 1973, 691-709.

"The manipulations of points of view force the reader as a

reader to share the problems of the characters as they seek order in the baffling world of THE WAVES".

336   Ridley, Hilda. "Leslie Stephen's Daughter", THE DALHOUSIE REVIEW, Halifax, Nova Scotia, XXXIII, No. 1, Spring 1953, 65-72.

Stresses Virginia Woolf's feminine approach to life--"the way of intuition and imagination" which she found in the character of her mother.

337   Rigo, G. de. "THE WAVES di Virginia Woolf", LETTERATURE MODERNE, 12: 1962.

338   Robb, Kenneth A. "Virginia Woolf's Miss Ormerod", AMERICAN NOTES AND QUERIES, New Haven, 7, 5, September 1968, p. 71.

Shows from textual evidence that Miss Ormerod does not appear in the English edition of THE COMMON READER, although it is included in the U.S. editions. Also, the word "Bos" in the same essay is a misprint for "Bot" which goes well with the next word "Warble".

339   Roberts, John Hawley. "Vision and Design in Virginia Woolf", PMLA, New York, Vol. 61, September 1946, pp. 835-847.

Discusses the influence of Roger Fry's aesthetics on Virginia Woolf. Mrs. Woolf rejected photographic representation and shared Fry's doctrine that the basic reaction to works of art is "a reaction to a relation and not to sensations or objects or persons or events". Examines MRS. DALLOWAY and TO THE LIGHTHOUSE in the light of this artistic creed.

340   _____. "Towards Virginia Woolf", THE VIRGINIA QUARTERLY REVIEW, Virginia, Vol. 10, October 1934, pp. 587-602.

Particularly good on Virginia Woolf's characterization. Refutes the conventional objection to Virginia Woolf's characterization. Declares that her purpose in all her novels is "to project the spirit we live by, life itself and her characters are not individuals but symbols created to illustrate that spirit".

341   Roberts, R. Ellis. "A Biographer Manqué", THE SATURDAY REVIEW OF LITERATURE, New York, October 3, 1942, p. 9.

Disagrees with the view that Virginia Woolf's range is limited and that she did not know "enough kinds of people".

342   Rogat, Ellen Hawkes. "The Virgin in the Bell Biography", TWENTIETH CENTURY LITERATURE, Denver, Colorado, Vol. 20, No. 2, April 1974, 96-113.

Questions Quenti Bell's opinion /VIRGINIA WOOLF: A BIOG-
RAPHY, Vol. II, 1972/ that Woolf's life and art had a "dis-
concertingly aetherial quality". Maintains that Woolf
"looked at and through everyday situations and perceived the
profound significance of social facts and personal relations".

343   _____. "Visiting the Berg Collection", VIRGINIA
WOOLF MISCELLANY, Stanford, 1,1, 1973, 1-2.

344   Roll-Hansen, Diderik. "Peter Walsh's Seven-League Boots: A
Note on MRS. DALLOWAY", ENGLISH STUDIES, Amsterdam, Vol. 50,
1969, 301-304.

Examines the time-scheme in MRS. DALLOWAY. Finds some defi-
ciencies in Woolf's handling of time in this novel.

345   Rosati, Salavatore. "Letterature Inglese: Virginia Woolf-
Aldous Huxley", NUOVA ANTOLOGIA, Rome, Vol. 370, December 16,
1933, 636-645.

A detailed analysis of the symbolism of ORLANDO.

346   _____. "Virginia Woolf", ENGLISH MISCÉLLANY, Rome,
I: 1950, 145-159.

347   Rosenbaum, S. P. "The Philosophical Realism of Virginia
Woolf", ENGLISH LITERATURE AND BRITISH PHILOSOPHY: A COLLEC-
TION OF ESSAYS, ed. S. P. Rosenbaum, Chicago and London,
1971, 316-56.

348   Rosenberg, Stuart. "The Match in the Crocus: Obtrusive Art
in Virginia Woolf's MRS. DALLOWAY", MODERN FICTION STUDIES,
Vol. XIII, No. 2, 1967, 211-220.

Argues that in MRS. DALLOWAY Virginia Woolf occasionally in-
trudes to indicate the transitions from one character to another. This she does when "she wishes to heighten aesthetic
unity".

349   Rubenstein, Roberta. "ORLANDO: Virginia Woolf's Improvisa-
tions on a Russian Theme", FORUM FOR MODERN LANGUAGE STUDIES,
Edinburgh, Vol. 9, April 1973, 166-169.

"Though nothing is 'simply one thing' in this fantasy-
biography/satire, one can speculate that Virginia Woolf is
mocking her own, as well as her contemporaries' period of
canonization of Russian literature".

350   _____. "Virginia Woolf and the Russian Point of
View", COMPARATIVE LITERATURE STUDIES, University of Illinois,
9: June 1972, 196-206.

"The emphasis on the 'semi-transparent envelope' of consciousness as well as the spiritual and subjective realms

of experience, the continuity between humour and pathos, the difficulty of true communication, the problem of loneliness and the question of life's ultimate meaning--all important aspects of Virginia Woolf's fiction derived at least encouragement, if not direct inspiration, from the fertilizing impact of Russian literature on her imagination".

351   _____. "The Evolution of an Image: Virginia Woolf and the 'Glove of Life'", ANTIGONISH REVIEW, Antigonish, Nova Scotia, 15: 1973, 43-50.

352   Russell, H. K. "Woolf's TO THE LIGHTHOUSE", THE EXPLICATOR, Virginia, VIII, March 1950, item 38.

"TO THE LIGHTHOUSE is a study of the feminine creative principle (embodied in Mrs. Ramsay) which in the midst of the flux ... unifies and sustains human personality despite the blind fecundity of nature on the one hand, and masculine analytical intellect on the other".

353   Sackville-West, Victoria. "The Landscape of a Mind", ENCOUNTER, Lond., 2: January 1954, 70-74.

Thinks that Virginia Woolf's oblique methods are appropriate for the elusive content of her novels.

354   _____. "Virginia Woolf and ORLANDO", THE LISTENER, Lond., January 27, 1955, 157-158.

Contains the letters Virginia Woolf wrote to Victoria Sackville-West when she was working on ORLANDO. They show the progress of the book at various stages.

355   Sakamoto, Kiminobo. "Mrs. Dalloway in Bond Street", EIGO SEINEN, Tokyo, 116: 1970, 524-526. /In Japanese/.

356   Sakamoto, Tadanobu. "ORLANDO: What Happened in it", HEROSHIMA STUDIES IN ENGLISH LANGUAGE AND LITERATURE, Tokyo, 19, 1, 1972, 22-23.

357   Samuels, Marilyn Schauner. "The Symbolic Functions of the Sun in MRS. DALLOWAY", MODERN FICTION STUDIES, 18: Autumn 1972, 387-399.

"The sun is the means by which the eye sees things clearly and figuratively, the means by which the soul envisions reality and truth. Bradshaw and Holmes reduce life to imprisonment in a shadowy cave; and it is Septimus alone who fully recognizes them for what they are--he alone has had direct exposure to the sun".

358   Samuelson, Ralph. "The Theme of MRS. DALLOWAY", CHICAGO REVIEW, Vol. 2, No. 1, IV, Winter 1958, pp. 57-76.

A powerful rebuttal of the charge of aesthetic dilettantism
against Virginia Woolf. Argues forcibly that Mrs. Woolf is
no mere aesthete. The content of her work is not insignificant. She discriminates between the different experiences
and actions of her characters and presents a definite attitude to life as she does in MRS. DALLOWAY, for instance,
whose theme is the conflict between the individual and so-
ciety--"the worth of individual personality and the need for
its expression".

359 _____. "Virginia Woolf, ORLANDO and the Feminist
Spirit", THE WESTERN HUMANITIES REVIEW, Utah, Vol. XV, No.
1, Winter 1961, pp. 51-58.

"At its best the feminist spirit in ORLANDO has nothing to
do with her (Virginia Woolf's) aggressive tendencies, but
shows her strong desires simply to be herself, to be true to
a point of view representative of some of the experiences and
feelings of her sex".

360 _____. "More Than One Room of Her Own: Virginia
Woolf's Critical Dilemmas", THE WESTERN HUMANITIES REVIEW,
Utah, Vol. XIX, No. 3, Summer 1965, pp. 249-256.

In her non-fiction Virginia Woolf is preoccupied with two
problems: "The problem of equality and difference between
the sexes" on the one hand, and "concern with class" on the
other. "She is a critic who is fiercely proud of both her
sex and upperclass, and yet she is a critic, and writer, who
tries hard now and then to break out of this double confine-
ment". This tension is a major motif in her essays. There
is no such tension in her novels where these problems are
dealt with intuitively rather than logically.

361 Savage, D. S. "Virginia Woolf", THE WITHERED BRANCH: SIX
STUDIES IN THE MODERN NOVEL, Lond., 1950, 70-105.

A most formidable attack on Woolf's work. Condemns a to-
tally 'aesthetic' approach to her and insists on the evaluation of her novels with reference to their content.

362 Schlack, Beverly Ann. "A Freudian Look at MRS. DALLOWAY",
LITERATURE AND PSYCHOLOGY (University of Hartford), 23: 1973,
49-58.

363 Schoff, Francis G. "Mrs. Dalloway and Mrs. Ramsay", IOWA
ENGLISH YEARBOOK (University of Iowa, School of Letters),
Vol. 9, Fall 1964, 54-60.

Focuses on the theme of alienation in Woolf's novels. Both
MRS. DALLOWAY and TO THE LIGHTHOUSE express "a bitter awareness that ... each man is indeed an island", and the moments
of contact are brief and feeble.

364   Schorer, Mark. "New Books in Review" (Rev. art.), THE YALE
       REVIEW, New Haven, Vol. 32, No. 2, December 1942, 377-381.

       Contends that Woolf over-emphasizes sensuous impressions
       and that she is unable to discriminate between various im-
       pressions because she has no coherent view of life.

365   Scott, George. "Virginia Woolf", THE ADELPHI, Lond., Vol.
       30, No. 2, February 1954, 169-176.

       A severe attack on Virginia Woolf's "preoccupation" with
       the inner life: she "luxuriates in self-concern to the ex-
       clusion of the outside world".

366   Segura, C. "The Transcendental and the Transitory in Vir-
       ginia Woolf's Novels", TWO STUDIES IN THE CONTEMPORARY NOVEL,
       Buenos Aires, 1943.

       Thinks that a characteristic feature of Virginia Woolf's
       style is her combination of the transcendental and the triv-
       ial. She often uses commonplace situations and ordinary
       words to achieve poetical effects.

367   Shanahan, Mary Steussy. "BETWEEN THE ACTS: Virginia Woolf's
       Final Endeavor in Art", TEXAS STUDIES IN LITERATURE AND LAN-
       GUAGE, Austin, Texas, Vol. XIV, No. 1, Spring 1972, 123-138.

       "BETWEEN THE ACTS can be seen as Mrs. Woolf's final effort
       to wrest a meaningful design out of the 'orts' and 'scraps'
       in a universe where civilized values have eroded...."

368   _____. "The Artist and the Resolution of THE WAVES",
       MODERN LANGUAGE QUARTERLY, Seattle, Washington, Vol. 36, No.
       1, March 1975.

369   Sharma, O. P. "Virginia Woolf's NIGHT AND DAY: A study in
       Feminist Assertion", THE INDIAN JOURNAL OF ENGLISH STUDIES,
       Calcutta, Vol. XII, 1971, 55-66. Suggests that by feminism
       Virginia Woolf did not mean the suffragist agitation for
       votes. She gave feminism "new psychological proportion and
       artistic nuances".

370   _____. "Feminism as Aesthetic Vision and Trans-
       cendance: A Study of Virginia Woolf's TO THE LIGHTHOUSE",
       PUNJAB UNIVERSITY RESEARCH BULLETIN (Arts) Chandigarh, Pun-
       jab, India, Vol. III, No. 1, April 1972, 1-8.

       "It is in the simultaneous completion of Lily's vision in
       art and her son's reaching the lighthouse that Mrs. Ramsay
       attains her spiritual transcendance as a woman and thereby
       symbolizes a new aesthetic feminism in this novel".

371   _____. "Feminism as Aesthetic Vision: A Study of
       Virginia Woolf's MRS. DALLOWAY", PUNJAB UNIVERSITY RESEARCH

BULLETIN (Arts), Chandigarh, Punjab, India, Vol. ii, No. ii, 1971, 1-10.

372   Shields, E. F. "Death and Individual Values in MRS. DAL-LOWAY", QUEEN'S QUARTERLY, Kingston, Ontario, 80: 1973, 79-89.

373   Shoukri, Doris E. C. "The Nature of Being in Woolf and Duras", CONTEMPORARY LITERATURE, Wisconsin, Vol. 12, No. 3, Summer 1971, 317-328.

Discusses Woolf's THE WAVES and Duras's THE RAVISHING OF LOL STEIN. These writers' concern with the nature of being leads them to consider "a similar set of problems: the relation of the individual psyche to others, to the collective unconscious and to the sea of eternity...."

374   Simon, Irène. "Some Aspects of Virginia Woolf's Imagery", ENGLISH STUDIES, Amsterdam, Vol. 41, No. 3, June 1966, 180-196.

A detailed study of Woolf's use of imagery in MRS. DALLOWAY and TO THE LIGHTHOUSE. Discusses the importance of the images as units in their structural pattern.

375   Smart, J. A. E. "Virginia Woolf", THE DALHOUSIE REVIEW, Halifax, Nova Scotia, Vol. XXI, 1941-1942, pp. 37-50.

A general survey of Woolf's work. Declares that "the purely formal qualities of her work are often so exquisite that she at last seems fascinated by her own power....Her work is marred by a distinct weakness of content. Her world is a limited world, a private world".

376   Smith, J. Oates. "Henry James and Virginia Woolf: The Art of Relationships", TWENTIETH CENTURY LITERATURE: A SCHOLARLY AND CRITICAL JOURNAL, Denver, Colorado, Vol. 10, No. 3, October 1964, pp. 119-129.

Believes that both James and Woolf think that "man gains his identity, /and/ experiences his 'life' in terms only of other people."

377   Somnath, A. "The Elegiac Strain in Virginia Woolf", JAMMU AND KASHMIR UNIVERSITY REVIEW, Srinagar, India, Vol. 1, 1958.

378   Spater, George A. "The Monks House Library", AMERICAN BOOK COLLECTOR, Chicago, Vol. 21, No. 4, January 1971, 18-20.

About the books on various subjects which the Woolfs had in their library at Monks House, Rodmell, Sussex.

379   Steele, Philip L. "Virginia Woolf's Spiritual Autobiography", TOPIC (Washington and Jefferson College), 9, 18, Fall 1969.

About ORLANDO. The book shows how in a "confused and tumultuous world" Woolf is trying to "discover the reality, the value, the meaning of life".

380   Steinberg, E. R. "Note on a Novelist Too Quickly Freudened", LITERATURE AND PSYCHOLOGY, New York, IV, 2, April 1954, 23-26.

A Freudian analysis of the significance of Peter Walsh's pocket knife in MRS. DALLOWAY.

381   Steinmann, Theo. "Virginia Woolf: TO THE LIGHTHOUSE, Die Doppelte Funktion der Malerin", DIE NEUEREN SPRACHEN, Frankfurt, 19, 11, November 1970, 537-547.

382   Stewart, Jack F. "Existence and Symbol in THE WAVES", MODERN FICTION STUDIES, 18: Autumn 1972, 433-447.

"Like Bernard, Virginia Woolf longs for an absolute that lies beyond the welter of sensations and for the necessary illusion of a form that gives order to eternal flux".

383   _____. "Historical Impressionism in ORLANDO", STUDIES IN THE NOVEL (North Texas State University), 5: 1973, 71-85.

384   Stewart, J. J. M. "Notes for a Study of THE WAVES", ON THE NOVEL: A PRESENT FOR WALTER ALLEN ON HIS 60TH BIRTH DAY FROM HIS FRIENDS AND COLLEAGUES, ed. B. S. Benedikz, Lond., 1971, 93-112.

"THE WAVES is about human isolation and the possibility of transcending that isolation. Mrs. Woolf says that our alienation is the consequence of our immersion in the stream of time, and that there come sacramental moments when time stands still. These moments are won through some spiritual discipline....It is a direct apprehension by the spirit of something not to be perceived by sense".

385   Strode, Hudson. "The Genius of Virginia Woolf" (Rev. art.), THE NEW YORK TIMES BOOK REVIEW, October 5, 1941, 1 and 30.

One of the finest appreciations of Virginia Woolf's writings. Gives high praise to her psychological insight and to her lyrical prose. "When one finishes a book of hers, it is not characters he remembers but their spiritual emanations, or facets of Virginia Woolf's supervision".

386   Summerhayes, Don. "Society, Morality, Analogy: Virginia Woolf's World Between the Acts", MODERN FICTION STUDIES, Vol. IX, No. 4, Winter 1963-64, pp. 329-337.

Argues that Virginia Woolf's concern in BETWEEN THE ACTS is with "such existential perceptions as those of psychic insularity, the oppressiveness of time, of the inability to communicate", and she has treated them aesthetically with the help of "interior monologue, recurrence of verbal motifs, and ironical detachment from direct statements of meaning".

387   Sutherland, J. R.   "Virginia Woolf", THE BRITISH WEEKLY, Lond., October 24, 1929, p. 81.

Thinks that what gives Virginia Woolf's work its distinction is the "queer sense of continuity, of life going on all the time in a hundred trivial ways flowing on endlessly and inconsequently and yet in a moving pattern...."

388   Swanston, H. F. G.   "Virginia Woolf and the Corinthians", NEW BLACKFRIARS, Oxford, Vol. 54, August 1973, 360-365.

389   Swinnerton, Frank.   "Virginia Woolf", THE GEORGIAN LITERARY SCENE: A PANORAMA, Lond., 1935, Chap. XII, p. 390.

Calls Virginia Woolf "essentially an impressionist, a catcher at memory of her own mental vagaries, and not a creator".

390   Szladits, Lola L.   "The Life, Character and Opinions of Flush the Spaniel", BULLETIN OF THE NEW YORK PUBLIC LIBRARY, New York, 74 , 4, April 1970, 211-218.

Thinks that Virginia Woolf chose Flush as a subject "because that particular dog's life gave a particular angle in a dog's eye view of what Elizabeth Barrett, tyrannized by a Victorian father, secluded in a bed-room, unvisited, and finally liberated by a man, would have necessarily felt".

391   Talamantes, Florence.   "Virginia Woolf and Alfonsina Storni: Kindred Spirits", VIRGINIA WOOLF QUARTERLY, San Diego,1,iii, 1973, 4-21.

392   Taylor, M. E.   "Virginia Woolf and the Novel", REVUE DE L'ENSEIGNEMENT DES LANGUES VIVANTES, Paris, Vol. 47, June 1930, 279-281.

Claims that Virginia Woolf is unparalleled in her success in "conveying to the reader the actual process of thinking".

393   Thackery, C. B.   "God and Mrs. Woolf", THE LONDON QUARTERLY AND HOLBORN REVIEW, Lond., January 1938, 96-99.

Maintains that Virginia Woolf is one of those who "set spiritual values above all others whether or not they confer a faith".

394   TIMES LITERARY SUPPLEMENT, London, April 12, 1941, p. 175, "Epitaph on Virginia Woolf: Interpreter of the Age Between the Wars.   The Vision and the Pursuit".

"Virginia Woolf took reality as she found it ... and tried

to make life stand still at the significant moment. It is
the aim of all great poets in every medium".

395   Tindall, William York. "Many-leveled Fiction: Virginia
       Woolf to Ross Lockridge", COLLEGE ENGLISH, Illinois, Vol. 10,
       No. 2, November 1948, 67-71.

       Finds in Woolf's novels different layers of meaning and sym-
       bol in the manner of the most successful practitioners of
       many-leveled fiction.

396   Toynbee, Philip. "Virginia Woolf: A Study of Three Experi-
       mental Novels", HORIZON, Lond., Vol. XIV, November 1946, 290-
       304.

       Largely unfavorable. Maintains that Virginia Woolf remained
       a lesser novelist than Joyce and James because her tools were
       inadequate. "She resolved to see only through the eyes of
       her characters. Her tragedy as an artist was that she could
       not do it and all her novels suffer from her stylistic uni-
       formity, and from the homogeneity of atmosphere which results
       from it".

397   Troy, William. "Virginia Woolf: The Poetic Method". THE
       SYMPOSIUM, New Hampshire, Vol. III, Jan-March   1932, 53-
       63, and "Virginia Woolf: The Poetic Style", Apr-June, 1932,
       153, 166   /Reprinted in M. D. Zabel, ed.,LITERARY OPINION IN
       AMERICA, New York, 1951, 324-337/.

       One of the major pieces of Woolf criticism in America. A
       close analysis of Mrs. Woolf's aesthetics. Complains that
       Mrs. Woolf's exclusive concentration on private conscious-
       ness has resulted in her detachment from concrete experience.
       She is overrefined. There is in her fiction no "active im-
       pact of character upon reality which provides the objective
       materials of experience in both literature and life".

398   _____. "Virginia Woolf and the Novel of Sensibil-
       ity", PERSPECTIVES, New York, Vol. 16, Winter 1954, 75-76.
       Reprinted in his SELECTED ESSAYS, New Brunswick, New Jersey,
       1967.

       A more favourable and sympathetic view of Virginia Woolf
       than his earlier verdict. "In re-reading the best of Mrs.
       Woolf's novels, one is to-day likely to be impressed by the
       vigour and zest about the whole essential business of human
       experience, amounting at moments to ecstasy".

399   Turnell, G. M. "Virginia Woolf", THE CAMBRIDGE REVIEW, Cam-
       bridge, England, October 19, 1928, pp. 29-30.

       Discusses, in general terms, Virginia Woolf's gifts and
       limitations as a novelist. Finds her most important con-
       tribution to fiction in the discovery of a new form which

enables her to 'get closer to life'--to probe man's hidden
thoughts and feelings. But her characters are vague spirits,
rather than robust and lively people.

400   Turnell, Martin. "Virginia Woolf", HORIZON, Lond., July 6,
       1942, pp. 44-56.

       Complains like the other 'moral' critics (Nos. 106; 286) that
       in Mrs. Woolf's work there are isolated moments of extraor-
       dinary vividness and beauty but she cannot co-ordinate these
       scattered impressions because she has no co-ordinated atti-
       tude to life, no conviction "that life is of a certain qual-
       ity".

401   _____. "The Shaping of Contemporary Literature:
       Lawrence, Forster, Virginia Woolf", MODERN LITERATURE AND
       CHRISTIAN FAITH, Lond., 1961, pp. 25-45.

       "The fundamental weakness of Forster's work, as of Virginia
       Woolf's, is a lack of faith. They believe in personal rela-
       tionships and tolerance and freedom but they are without any
       clear conception of the Good Life".

402   Warner, John M. "Symbolic Patterns of Retreat and Reconcili-
       ation in TO THE LIGHTHOUSE". DISCOURSE: A REVIEW OF THE
       LIBERAL ARTS (Minnesota College, Muirhead), Vol. 12: 1969,
       376-392.

       Thinks that TO THE LIGHTHOUSE is a symbolic statement of "the
       artist's problem to find the balance" between "the realities
       of the inner and outer worlds".

403   Warren, Ramsay. "The Claims of Language: Virginia Woolf as
       Symbolist", THE ENGLISH FICTION IN TRANSITION, Lafayette,
       Indiana, Vol. 4, No. 1, 1961, 12-16.

       Shows how like the symbolists Woolf uses certain recurrent
       symbols in her novels.

404   Watkins, Renée. "Survival in Discontinuity: Virginia Woolf's
       BETWEEN THE ACTS", THE MASSACHUSETTS REVIEW, Vol. X, No. 2,
       Spring 1969, 356-376.

       Discusses BETWEEN THE ACTS against the contemporary back-
       ground. Thinks that Woolf shows through the village pageant
       "the threatened English community" without "any shared body
       of deep beliefs" and "clear ideas".

405   Webb, Igor. "Things in Themselves: Virginia Woolf's THE
       WAVES", MODERN FICTION STUDIES, Lafayette, Indiana, Vol. XVII,
       No. 4, Winter 1971-72, pp. 570-573.

       Argues that in THE WAVES Virginia Woolf attempts to show that
       the senses are the "conveyors of reality". The conscious

57

self or the ego is a "blinder" which "distorts the immediacy of sensuous life". Bernard experiences "things in themselves", without trying to "incorporate sensuous reality into a subjective vision".

406   Wellesley, Dorothy.   "Virginia", THE VIRGINIA QUARTERLY REVIEW, Vol. 20, Winter 1944, pp. 60-61.

A laudatory poem on Virginia Woolf.

407   Whitehead, L. M.   "The Shawl and the Skull: Virginia Woolf's 'Magic Mountain'", MODERN FICTION STUDIES, 18: Autumn 1972, 401-415.

Thinks that in wrapping her shawl about the skull Mrs. Ramsay hides "the knowledge of death, terror and dissolution behind a veil... in this case the illusion of a magic mountain. The magic mountain is a symbol for all of man's imaginative and spiritual creations of which 'art' is the paradigm.... The wealth of reverberations and overtones of the image of the shawl and the skull lead finally to an elegiac vision, a celebration not of life against death, but of life with its roots in death".

408   Wilkinson, Ann Yanko.   "A Principle of Unity in BETWEEN THE ACTS", CRITICISM: A QUARTERLY FOR LITERATURE AND THE ARTS, Wayne State University Press, Detroit, Vol. 8, No. 1, Winter 1966, pp. 53-63.

Maintains that BETWEEN THE ACTS does not lack unity. One finds the principle of unity everywhere in the novel. "The drama in BETWEEN THE ACTS consists not only in the conflict of opposites but in the more startling revelation of the identity of these opposites: isolation and connection, permanence and mutability, stasis and flow, appearance and reality".

409   Williams, Orlo.   "TO THE LIGHTHOUSE" (Rev. art.), THE CRITERION, Lond., Vol. VI, No. 1, July 1927, p. 28.

Questions the validity of Virginia Woolf's fictional method, because 'making of the moment something permanent' is the work of the poet, not of the novelist.

410   Wilson, Angus.   "A WRITER'S DIARY" (Rev. art.), THE OBSERVER, Lond., November 1, 1953, p. 9.

Complains that there is in Virginia Woolf's novels "confusion of values" and "an overweight of imagery" that has had a most harmful effect upon subsequent writing.

411   _____.   "Evil in the English Novel: From George Eliot to Virginia Woolf", THE LISTENER, Lond., January 3, 1963, p. 16.

Comments on Virginia Woolf's treatment of evil in THE WAVES
and BETWEEN THE ACTS.

412 Wilson, Edmund. "Virginia Woolf and Logan Pearsall-Smith",
THE NEW YORKER, May 27, 1950.

413 _____. "Virginia Woolf and the American Language",
THE SHORES OF LIGHT: A LITERARY CHRONICLE OF THE TWENTIES
AND THIRTIES, New York, 1952, 421-426.

On the controversy in the NEW REPUBLIC over Virginia Woolf's
views on American English.

414 Wilson, James Southall. "Time and Virginia Woolf", THE VIR-
GINIA QUARTERLY REVIEW, Virginia, Vol. 18, No. 1, Winter 1942,
pp. 267-276.

Another valuable viewpoint on Mrs. Woolf's concept of time.
Shows how in her novels time and human consciousness are in-
terrelated. Time "has meaning only in terms of human experience" and is "not important in what it can do objectively or
physically".

415 Woolf, Leonard. "Virginia Woolf: Writer and Personality",
THE LISTENER, London, March 4, 1965, pp. 327-328.

Maintains that Virginia Woolf was not aloof from the society
around her. She was "social with every kind of person, because she was interested in what was going on in a person's
mind".

416 _____. "Virginia Woolf and THE WAVES", RADIO TIMES,
Lond., June 23, 1957, p. 25.

Calls THE WAVES Virginia Woolf's masterpiece, because "it
does succeed in showing the relation of six real persons to
the most important things in human existence: friendship,
love, life and death".

417 _____. "A Note on Virginia Woolf's NIGHT AND DAY",
SOUTHERLY, Sidney, December 1942, pp. 10-11.

Contests the view that NIGHT AND DAY antedated THE VOYAGE
OUT. Thinks that while writing THE VOYAGE OUT Virginia
Woolf was dissatisfied with the traditional form of the
novel and began to feel her way towards a new craft. Because she had not yet learnt her experimental technique well
enough, Mrs. Woolf wrote NIGHT AND DAY on conventional lines
as a 'necessary stage' in her artistic development.

418 _____. "Génie et folie de Virginia Woolf", REVUE
DE PARIS, Vol. 72, July-August 1965, 91-111.

419 Wright, Nathalie. "MRS. DALLOWAY: A Study in Composition",

COLLEGE ENGLISH, Illinois, V, April 1944, pp. 351-355.

Attempts to show how the use of some recurrent 'patterns'--
psychological states, colour, sound,etc.--serves to give the
novel its unity and synthesis. This juxtaposition of patterns is "one of Mrs. Woolf's most brilliant achievements".

420   Wyatt, F. "Some Comments on the Use of Symbols in the Novel",
      LITERATURE AND PSYCHOLOGY, New York, Vol. 4, No. 2, pp. 15-23.

      On the symbolic significance of Peter Walsh's pocket knife in
      MRS. DALLOWAY.

421   Wyatt, Jean M. "MRS. DALLOWAY: Literary Allusion as Struc-
      tural Metaphor",PMLA, New York, Vol. 88, No. 3, May 1973,
      440-451.

      Analyses in detail the text of MRS. DALLOWAY to show how Vir-
      ginia Woolf draws on various allusions in order to give the
      novel its thematic and structural unity. "Virginia Woolf
      interweaves allusion and image to construct character, define
      theme and structure MRS. DALLOWAY".

422   Yourcenar, M. "Sur Virginia Woolf", IMPRESSIONS, Paris, 5:
      1938 (Special No. on Virginia Woolf).

423   _____. "Une femme etincelante et timide", ADAM
      INTERNATIONAL REVIEW, Lond., 364-366, 1972, 16-17.

424   Zorn, Marilyn. "The Pageant in BETWEEN THE ACTS", MODERN
      FICTION STUDIES, Vol. 2, No. 1, February 1956, 31-35.

      Shows how the pageant emphasizes the central theme of BE-
      TWEEN THE ACTS. Regards it as a "vehicle for releasing the
      individual from the burden of his aloneness, his absorption
      in the ego and time, and his subjection to change".

425   Zuckerman, Joanne P. "Anne Thackeray Ritchie as the Model
      for Mrs. Hilbery in Virginia Woolf's NIGHT AND DAY", VIR-
      GINIA WOOLF QUARTERLY, San Diego, Spring 1973, 32-46.

III.   INTRODUCTIONS AND PREFACES BY EDITORS IN SELECTIONS

FROM VIRGINIA WOOLF

426   Guiguet, Jean.   Preface to CONTEMPORARY WRITERS by Virginia
      Woolf, 1965, pp. 7-12.

      A collection of Virginia Woolf's essays and reviews which
      appeared mostly in the TIMES LITERARY SUPPLEMENT between
      1905 and 1921. These essays shed light on Woolf's own
      theory and practice as a novelist.

427   Hoare, D. M.   Introduction to TO THE LIGHTHOUSE (Everyman's
      Library Edition), 1955, pp. V-X.

      Hoare thinks that TO THE LIGHTHOUSE makes explicit one of
      the major themes in Virginia Woolf's fiction which had been
      implicit in her earlier novels: that there is no conflict
      between life and art. The problem of both is to "make the
      moment perfect, to harmonize discords, to attain a central
      significance".

428   James, Walter.   Introduction to VIRGINIA WOOLF: SELECTIONS
      FROM HER ESSAYS, 1966, pp. 7-20.

      James argues, unlike the SCRUTINEERS, that to seek truth or
      reality was Virginia Woolf's one aim and what she detested
      most in literature and society was falsehood and a distortion
      of reality. As a social and literary critic Mrs. Woolf in-
      sisted on an "accurate representation of life", but because
      of the contemporary break-down of "a framework of commonly
      held beliefs", she sought truth or reality in her own emo-
      tions.

IV MEMOIRS, OBITUARY NOTICES AND ARTICLES

(a) MEMOIRS

429   Bell, Clive. OLD FRIENDS, Lond., 1956, p. 95.

Speaks of Virginia Woolf's 'pure' vision and of her relationship with the French Impressionists.

430   Bell, Quentin. "Magisterial", THE LISTENER, Lond., February 26, 1970, p. 278.

From Quentin Bell's interview in a B B C Third Programme.
Replying to the question whether Leonard Woolf was aware
of the mental condition of his wife at the time of their
engagement, Bell says that Leonard did not know 'just how
bad it had been'.

431   Blanche, Jacques-Emile. MORE PORTRAITS OF A LIFE-TIME 1918-
1938, Lond., 1939.

Recalls how he enjoyed THE YEARS and wrote to Virginia
Woolf about his appreciation of the novel.

432   Cecil, David. DICTIONARY OF NATIONAL BIOGRAPHY 1941-1950,
p. 975.

Speaks from personal knowledge of Virginia Woolf's sheltered
childhood, her lack of University education, association
with the Bloomsbury Group and her nervous break-downs.

433   Easdale, G. E. MIDDLE AGE 1895-1932 (An Autobiography),
Lond., 1935.

Mrs. Easdale recalls her impression about Virginia Woolf:
'a kind and gracious' lady who had a delicious wit.

434   Garnett, David. "Keynes, Strachey and Virginia Woolf in
1917", THE LONDON MAGAZINE, Vol. 2, No. 9, September 1955,
48-55.

Garnett recalls how he was excited by the experiments of
Virginia Woolf.

435   _____. THE FLOWERS OF THE FOREST, Lond., 1965,
161-162. Also about Woolf's experiments with fiction.

436   Harrod, R. F. THE LIFE OF JOHN MAYNARD KEYNES, Lond.,
       1951, 172-178.

       Speaks of Keynes's praise for Virginia Woolf's "sensitiv-
       ity, deep psychology and great humanity".

437   Hart-Davis, Rupert. HUGH WALPOLE: A BIOGRAPHY, Lond.,
       1952, 289-290.

       When ORLANDO was published, Hugh Walpole declared, "What a
       book! . . . This marks the difference between genius and
       talent. ORLANDO is all genius".

438   Holroyd, Michael. LYTTON STRACHEY: A CRITICAL BIOGRAPHY:
       THE UNKNOWN YEARS 1880-1910, 1967, p. 435.

       Holroyd describes the relationship between Virginia Woolf
       and Lytton Strachey. Strachey "admired" Mrs. Woolf though
       her novels "were not to his taste".

439   Isherwood, Christopher. "Virginia Woolf", DECISION, New
       York, May 1941, 36-38.

       Recalls his meeting with Virginia Woolf.

440   Lehmann, John. "Working with Virginia Woolf", THE LISTENER,
       January 13, 1955, pp. 60-62.

       Sometime manager at the Woolfs' Hogarth Press, Lehmann re-
       calls in this article his memories of Mrs. Woolf as a pub-
       lisher and writer.

441   _____. THE WHISPERING GALLERY: AUTOBIOGRAPHY I,
       1955, pp. 168-172.

       Speaks of the contemporary significance of Virginia Woolf's
       novels--JACOB'S ROOM, MRS. DALLOWAY and TO THE LIGHTHOUSE,
       in particular.

442   _____. I AM MY BROTHER: AUTOBIOGRAPHY II, 1960,
       pp. 33-35, 112-118 and passim.

       About Lehmann's occasional meetings with Mrs. Woolf and his
       talks with her on books and writers. Quotes the letter she
       wrote to him asking his opinion on the manuscript of her
       novel BETWEEN THE ACTS.

443   (THE) LISTENER, January 15, 1970, pp. 87-88 ("The Death
      of Virginia Woolf").

      The recollections of Elizabeth Bowen, Angelica Garnett
      (Virginia Woolf's niece) and Louie Mayer (the Woolfs'
      housekeeper) of the last days of Mrs. Woolf. Although
      these days were very sad for her and she was under severe
      strain, nevertheless Mrs. Woolf sometimes showed 'a cap-
      acity for joy'.

444   Mackenzie, Compton. MY LIFE AND TIMES, 1931-1938, Lond.,
      1968, 36-37.

      Mackenzie recalls how deeply he was impressed by THE WAVES.

445   Plomer, William. AT HOME: MEMORIES, Lond., 1958, pp.
      50-58.

      Maintains that Virginia Woolf was not cut off from social
      life: "In each of us there are two beings: one solitary,
      one social. In Virginia Woolf the two beings seemed to
      have an equal life and so to make her into a complete per-
      son".

446   Roberts, R. E. "Virginia Woolf 1882-1941", SATURDAY RE-
      VIEW OF LITERATURE, New York, April 12, 1941.

447   Spender, Stephen. WORLD WITHIN WORLD: THE AUTOBIOGRAPHY
      OF STEPHEN SPENDER, 1951, p. 164.

      Recalls what Virginia Woolf had once said to him about her
      idea of the novel:
      "I don't think there is any form in which the novel has to
      be written. My idea is to make use of every form and bring
      it within a unity which is that particular novel.. . . I
      would like to write a novel which is a fusion of poetry
      and dialogue as in a play. I would like to experiment in
      every form and bring it within the scope of the novel".

448   Trautmann, Joanne. "A Talk with Nigel Nicolson", VIRGINIA
      WOOLF QUARTERLY, 1, 1, Fall, 1972, 38-44.

      Nigel Nicolson, son of Victoria Sackville-West, recalls
      the relationship between Virginia Woolf and his mother.

449   Walpole, Hugh. EXTRACTS FROM A DIARY, Glasgow, 1934, 67-68.

Thinks that Arnold Bennett disliked Virginia Woolf because he "had no sense of any world beyond this one. Everything in his view was bounded by bricks and mortar".

450   Wells, H. G. EXPERIMENT IN AUTOBIOGRAPHY, Vol. II, Lond., 1934, p. 462.

Wells speaks of his dislike for Virginia Woolf's work.

451   West, Rebecca. ENDING IN EARNEST, New York, 1931, pp. pp. 208-213.

Recalls the immediate popularity of Virginia Woolf's ORLANDO.

452   Wilson, Edmund. "Meetings with Max Beerbohm 1873-1956", ENCOUNTER, December 1963, 19-20.

Refers to Max's dislike of Virginia Woolf's novels.

453   Woolf, Leonard. SOWING: AN AUTOBIOGRAPHY OF THE YEARS 1880-1904, Lond., 1960, pp. 180-186.

Describes his first meeting with Virginia Stephen. Refers to Mr. Ramsay's resemblance to Leslie Stephen. Thinks that in spite of the similarity the portrait of Mr. Ramsay in TO THE LIGHTHOUSE is exaggerated.

454   _____. BEGINNING AGAIN: AN AUTOBIOGRAPHY OF THE YEARS 1911-1918, 1964, pp. 28-33, 149-166, 172-173, passim.

About Leonard's marriage with Virginia and her mental illness at different times.

455   _____. DOWNHILL ALL THE WAY: AN AUTOBIOGRAPHY OF THE YEARS 1919 TO 1939, 1967.

Mentions the various aspects of Virginia Woolf's life and personality: her sensitivity to criticism of her work, her worry about the fate of her books, her earnings, her friendship with T. S. Eliot and Victoria Sackville-West, and the contemporary success of some of her books such as ORLANDO, FLUSH, and THE YEARS.

456   _____. THE JOURNEY NOT THE ARRIVAL MATTERS: AN AUTOBIOGRAPHY OF THE YEARS 1939 to 1969, Lond., 1970.

Gives a pathetic account of Virginia Woolf's acute depressions which resulted in her suicide.

(b)   OBITUARY NOTICES AND ARTICLES

457   Baker, Margaret. "Virginia Woolf", THE ADELPHI, May 1941,
      pp. 294-295.

458   Cecil, Lord David. "A Note on Virginia Woolf", TIME AND
      TIDE, Lond., May 17, 1941, pp. 395-396.

      Regards Virginia Woolf as an aesthete: "Far more success-
      fully than any professional poet has she revealed the
      aesthetic quality in the modern scene".

459   (THE) CHRISTIAN CENTURY, Chicago, May 7, 1941, p. 632.

      ("Tragic Death of Novelist")
      Warm praise for Virginia Woolf's imagination and 'integrity
      of mind'.

460   Eliot, T. S. "Virginia Woolf", HORIZON, London, Vol. III,
      May 1941, pp. 313-316.

      High praise for Mrs. Woolf. Eliot declares that Mrs. Woolf
      represented a unique "pattern of culture" and she was "the
      centre, not merely of an esoteric group, but of the literary
      life of London".

461   Evans, Ifor B.   "Virginia Woolf", THE MANCHESTER GUARDIAN,
      April 4, 1941, p. 10.

      Appreciates Virginia Woolf's sensitivity and her mastery of
      language.

462   Garnett, David. "Virginia Woolf", THE NEW STATESMAN AND
      NATION, April 12, 1941, p. 386.

      Admires Virginia Woolf's success in expressing sensitive
      response to the 'multiplicity of events' in language which
      is equally sensitive and poetic.

463   Grant, Duncan. "Virginia Woolf", HORIZON, Lond., Vol. III,
      June 1941, 402-406.

      Speaks of Virginia Woolf's likes and dislikes, habits and
      attitudes and her friendship with the Bloomsbury Group.

464   J. R. A. "Virginia Woolf", THE NEW YORK TIMES, October 5,
       1941, p. 2.

       An appreciation of Virginia Woolf's contributions to the
       English novel.

465   Lady Oxford. "Virginia Woolf", THE TIMES, London, April
       9, 1941, p. 7.

       Speaks highly of Virginia Woolf's rare imaginative gift.

466   Lehmann, Rosamond. "For Virginia Woolf", NEW WRITING,
       Lond., June 1941, pp. 53-58.

       Describes Mrs. Woolf's physical and intellectual char-
       acteristics: "She was in herself, in her person, a per-
       fectly poetic creature" who was "intensely aware of the
       spiritual reality of human beings".

467   Macaulay, Rose. "Virginia Woolf", THE SPECTATOR, Lond.,
       April 11, 1941. p. 394.

       Virginia Woolf had a "zest for actual life and actual peo-
       ple" and "little in humanity was alien to her and not much
       outside it."

468   _____. "Virginia Woolf", HORIZON, Lond., Vol.
       III, May 1941, pp. 316-318.

       "Animation, sensibility, zest, sympathy, imagination, wit,
       irony and culture--all these combined in Virginia Woolf to
       make a person so rare and so delightful that she is not to
       be met elsewhere at all."

469   MacCarthy, Desmond. "Virginia Woolf", THE SUNDAY TIMES,
       London, April 6, 1941, p. 8.

       Praises Virginia Woolf's contribution to the English novel.

470   (THE) NEW REPUBLIC, New York, April 14, 1941, p. 487 (the
       editorial).

       Mrs. Woolf's novels "make a demand on the reader like that
       of poetry of the first order."

471   Paterson, Isabel. "The Vitality That was Virginia Woolf:
       Curbed But Indestructible; It Touched the Secret of Being",

NEW YORK TRIBUNE, July 13, 1941, pp. 1-2.

Mrs. Woolf did not merely trace the flow of consciousness, she touched the "secret of pure being."

472   Plomer, William. "Virginia Woolf", HORIZON, Lond., Vol. III, May 1941, 323-327.

Thinks that Virginia Woolf did not live in an ivory tower. Her life was rich in experience of people and places.

473   Roberts, R. Ellis. "Virginia Woolf", THE SATURDAY REVIEW OF LITERATURE, New York, April 12, 1941, pp. 12 and 19.

"The supremacy of Virginia Woolf was acknowledged partly because she was so essentially a feminine author. And her feminism was of the sound, old-fashioned Victorian kind—the kind of feminism which takes its stand on the inexpungable thesis that a woman has a right, a duty to claim certain privileges because she is a woman".

474   Selincourt, Basil de. "Virginia Woolf. An Appreciation", THE OBSERVER, London, April 16, 1941, p. 5.

". . . the reading of her novels can be a strenuous exercise, but it is an exercise in intimacy".

475   Smith, L. P. "Tavistock Square," ORION, Lond., Vol 2, Autumn 1945, 73-86.

Thinks that it is as a letter-writer that Virginia Woolf will be chiefly remembered.

476   Spender, Stephen. "Virginia Woolf. A Tribute," THE LISTENER, Lond., April 10, 1941, p. 533.

"To have known Virginia Woolf is a great privilege, because it is to have known an extraordinary and poetic and beautiful human being."

477   Taylor, John. "A School Boy's Tribute," THE SPECTATOR, Lond., April 11, 1941, p. 394.

A little poem about Virginia Woolf. Deals with her agony in a world of "man-born strife" in which she saw herself.

478   TIME AND TIDE, Lond., April 12, 1941, p. 306.

Maintains that Virginia Woolf "never lost sight of her human responsibility as an artist to communicate with her fellow creatures, never allowed herself to stray off into a private world."

479   TIMES LITERARY SUPPLEMENT, Lond., April 12, 1941, p. 179. ("End of an Epoch")

Claims that Virginia Woolf was "unparalleled in her heroic integrity in pursuing the Herculean vision of a fleeting universe".

480   Trevelyan, R. C. "Virginia Woolf", THE ABINGER CHRONICLE, London, Apr-May 1941, 23-24.

Describes the characteristics of Virginia Woolf's novels.

481   Walpole, Hugh. "Virginia Woolf", THE NEW STATESMAN AND NATION, Lond., XXI, June 14, 1941, 602-603.

Found in Mrs. Woolf a "kindliness of heart and tenderness of feeling" which was "rich with an intense personal charity".

V CORRESPONDENCE, LETTERS TO THE EDITOR AND INTERVIEWS

(a) CORRESPONDENCE

482 Collet, Georges-Paul. "Jacques-Emile Blanche and Virginia
Woolf", COMPARATIVE LITERATURE, Eugene, Oregon, Vol. xvii,
No. 1, Winter 1965, pp. 73-81.

Collet quotes the Virginia Woolf-Jacques Emile Blanche correspondence on TO THE LIGHTHOUSE, ORLANDO and THE WAVES.

483 Forster, E. M. GOLDSWORTHY LOWES DICKINSON, Lond., 1962,
pp. 230 & 233.

Forster quotes the enthusiastic letters of Goldsworthy
Lowes Dickinson, the Cambridge philosopher and humanist, to
Virginia Woolf about her novel THE WAVES.

484 Huxley, Aldous. Letter to Robert Nicholas dated 17th
February 1930, quoted in Grover Smith, LETTERS OF ALDOUS
HUXLEY, Lond., 1969, p. 330.

The letter shows Huxley's unfavourable response to TO THE
LIGHTHOUSE. Huxley complains of Mrs. Woolf's 'remoteness'
from real life.

485 Macaulay, Rose. LETTERS TO A FRIEND 1950-1952, Lond.,
1961, p. 315.

Tells her cousin John Hamilton Cowper Johnson about her
great devotion to and admiration for Virginia Woolf.

486 _____. LAST LETTERS TO A FRIEND 1952-1958, Lond.,
1962, pp. 141-143, 249.

487 Mansfield, Katherine. KATHERINE MANSFIELD'S LETTERS TO
J. M. MURRY 1913-1922, ed. J. M. Murry, 1951 (Letters
dated November 13 and 25, 1919).

The letters describe Katherine Mansfield's unfavourable
reactions to Mrs. Woolf's novel NIGHT AND DAY.

488 _____. THE LETTERS OF KATHERINE MANSFIELD, ed.
John Middleton Murry, Hamburg, 1934, Letters dated August
1917 and May 1918. The first letter praises THE MARK ON
THE WALL and the second KEW GARDENS.

489   Rothenstein, William. SINCE FIFTY: MEN AND MEMORIES 1922-
       1938, Lond., p. 277.

       Quotes from Virginia Woolf's letter to him about criticism.

490   Sanger, Charles Percy. Unpublished correspondence between
       Virginia Woolf and Charles Percy Sanger, quoted in VIRGINIA
       WOOLF by Dorothy Brewster, 1963, pp. 162-163.

       In three letters to Charles Percy Sanger, Mrs. Woolf tells
       him how she feels about her experiments in JACOB'S ROOM,
       MRS. DALLOWAY and TO THE LIGHTHOUSE.

491   Shaw, G. B. Letter to Virginia Woolf dated 10th May, 1940,
       quoted in BEGINNING AGAIN by Leonard Woolf, pp. 125-126.

       Shaw recalls his first meeting with Mrs. Woolf in a house
       in Sussex and its association with his play HEARTBREAK
       HOUSE.

492   Smith, L. P. "Tavistock Square", ORION, Lond., Autumn
       1945, p. 76.

       Quotes Virginia Woolf's letter to him about JACOB'S ROOM.

493   Strachey, Lytton. Letter to Virginia Woolf, dated October
       9, 1922, quoted in VIRGINIA WOOLF & LYTTON STRACHEY LETTERS,
       ed. Leonard Woolf and James Strachey, 1956, 103-4.

       Contains Strachey's views on JACOB'S ROOM.

494   Woolf, Leonard. Letter to Professor Erwin Steinberg, "Note
       on a Note", LITERATURE AND PSYCHOLOGY, New York, Vol. 4,
       No. 4, September 1954, p. 61.

       Mr. Woolf informs Professor Steinberg that Mrs. Woolf did
       not read much of Freud and the symbols regarding Peter
       Walsh's pocket knife in MRS. DALLOWAY are not Freudian.

       (b) LETTERS TO THE EDITOR

495   Cecil, David. "Virginia Woolf", Letter to the Editor, THE
       TIMES LITERARY SUPPLEMENT, April 19, 1941, p. 191.

       Maintains that Virginia Woolf's work, far from "dishearten-
       ing", is most "strengthening to the spirit", because "she

discovered beauty in things hitherto looked on as ugly and prosaic".

496   Daniels, Earl. Letter to the Editor, THE SATURDAY REVIEW, New York, December 5, 1931, p. 352.

About THE WAVES. "The value of THE WAVES is in its significant presentation . . . of what literature . . . has always regarded as of first importance; man in the midst of things, man set upon by things, man confused, facing that inner real self of whose existence he feels sure".

497   Lewis, Wyndham. Letter to the Editor, THE SPECTATOR, Lond., November 2, 1934.

Lewis accuses Mrs. Woolf of "puerile imitation" of Joyce's ULYSSES in MRS. DALLOWAY.

(c) INTERVIEWS

498   Compton-Burnett, Ivy. "Interviews with Ivy Compton-Burnett," A REVIEW OF ENGLISH LITERATURE, Lond., Vol. 3, No. 4, October 1962, p. 103.

Contains Miss Compton-Burnett's opinion about Virginia Woolf's novels. According to her, Mrs. Woolf is not a 'good' novelist, because she can neither create full-blooded characters nor handle the tough actualities of life.

499   Fry, Phillip and James W. Lee. "An Interview in Austin with John Lehmann", STUDIES IN THE NOVEL, 3, 1, September 1971, 80-96.

Lehmann remarks on Virginia Woolf's poetic use of the novel.

500   Ratcliffe, Michael. "The Ghost Lives," THE TIMES, Lond., January 19, 1970.

501   Snow, C. P. "Interview with C. P. Snow," A REVIEW OF ENGLISH LITERATURE, Lond., July 1962, p. 105.

Asserts that the "aestheticism" of Virginia Woolf and Joyce has "little meaning and no future".

502   Watts, Janet. "Dear Quentin: Janet Watts Interviews Mr. Bell of Bloomsbury", VIRGINIA WOOLF QUARTERLY, San Diego,

California, 1, 1, Fall, 1972 111-116. Reprinted from the ARTS GUARDIAN, Lond., June 14, 1972.

Quentin Bell discusses his biography of Virginia Woolf.

VI   GENERAL WORKS

(Listed below are books and articles which contain observations on Virginia Woolf's work)

503   Albert, Edward. A HISTORY OF ENGLISH LITERATURE, Lond.,
      1955, pp. 516-520.

504   Allen, Walter. THE ENGLISH NOVEL: A SHORT CRITICAL HISTORY,
      Lond., 1954, 329-337.

      Complains about Woolf's 'lack' of broad human contacts and
      her 'preoccupation' with sensibility.

505   Anderson, James. BRITISH NOVELS OF THE TWENTIETH CENTURY,
      Lond., 1959, p. 27.

      Calls TO THE LIGHTHOUSE one of the twentieth century novels
      which "by their style, imaginative power, or social
      interest, have some claim to a permanent place on the
      shelves of a personal library".

506   Annan, Noel. LESLIE STEPHEN: HIS THOUGHT AND CHARACTER
      IN RELATION TO HIS TIME, Lond., 1951, pp. 98-99.

      Shows how Mr. Ramsay in TO THE LIGHTHOUSE is a true portrait
      of Leslie Stephen.

507   Baldeshwiler, Eileen. "The Lyric Short Story: The Sketch
      of a History", STUDIES IN SHORT FICTION, Newberry College,
      South Carolina, 6, 4, Summer 1969, 443-453.

      Discusses the new mode in the short stories of Virginia
      Woolf. Shows how Woolf uses new language and new struc-
      tures because the emphasis of her stories is on the states
      of mind and on the delicate analysis of subtle moods. She
      traces "with the diction and rhythms of the poet the fall
      of the atoms on the mind".

508   Beach, J. W. THE TWENTIETH CENTURY NOVEL, New York, 1932,
      490-500.

      Maintains that Virginia Woolf does not believe in art for
      art's sake, and that her work is not removed from the "pri-
      mary interests of men".

74

509   Beckson, Karl and Munro, John M. "Symons, Browning and the
       Development of the Modern Aesthetic," STUDIES IN ENGLISH
       LITERATURE, p. 10, 4, Autumn 1970, 687-699.

       About Symons's influence on Woolf. The critics suggest
       that Symons anticipated the aesthetic of Woolf's fiction.

510   Beja, Morris. EPIPHANY IN THE MODERN NOVEL, Seattle, Wash-
       ington, 1971.

       The novelists discussed are Virginia Woolf, Joyce, Thomas
       Wolfe and Faulkner.

511   Bell, Clive. "What was Bloomsbury?" THE TWENTIETH CENTURY,
       Lond., February 1954, 153-160.

       About the origin of the Bloomsbury Group.

512   Bell, Quentin. BLOOMSBURY, Lond., 1968, 26-27, 96-98.

       Virginia Woolf's nephew and son of Clive Bell gives an
       authentic account of the intellectual and artistic life of
       Bloomsbury. Speaks of Mrs. Woolf's keen interest in the
       visual arts and of her idea of reality as something to be
       apprehended "by way of intuition and sensibility".

513   Bennett, Arnold. THINGS THAT HAVE INTERESTED ME, Third
       series, Lond., 1926, 193-194.

       Condemns Virginia Woolf's characterization in MRS. DALLOWAY.

514   _____.THE SAVOUR OF LIFE: ESSAYS IN GUSTO, Lond.,
       1928, 47-49, 253-54.

       Finds two defects in Woolf's fiction:
       (a) insubstantial characterization
       (b) amorphous construction.

514a   _____ ."The Progress of the Novel", THE REALIST,
       Lond., April 1929, p. 10.

       Does not agree with the opinion that Virginia Woolf was a
       great innovator in modern fiction: "her alleged form is
       the absence of form ...."

515   Benson, E. F. "Two Types of Modern Fiction", THE LONDON
       MERCURY, February 1928, 423.

Criticizes the stream of consciousness in MRS. DALLOWAY.

516   Benstock, Bernard. "The Present Recaptured: D. H. Lawrence and Others", THE SOUTHERN REVIEW, Baton Rouge, Louisiana, 4, 3, Summer 1968, 802-816.

Thinks that Virginia Woolf's analyses of human personality are limited and, therefore, unsatisfactory.

517   Bentley, Phyllis. SOME OBSERVATIONS ON THE ART OF NARRATIVE, Lond., 1946, 34-38.

Claims that Woolf has opened up a new possibility for the craft of fiction: the use of 'scene' instead of 'summary', the emphasis on single, specific moments in a character's life rather than on a continuous narrative.

518   Bloomfield, Paul. "Bloomsbury", THE ADELPHI, Lond., November 1954, 11-26, Reproduced in his UNCOMMON PEOPLE: A STUDY OF ENGLAND'S ELITE, Lond., 1955, 142-143.

"Although Virginia Woolf often aimed at saying what she had to say not in so many words, she was not in flight from objectivity, but in a sense doing for prose fiction what the French Impressionists had done for painting".

519   Blotner, Joseph. CYCLOPAEDIA OF WORLD AUTHORS, ed. F. N. Magill, New York, 1958, p. 1171.

Brief discussions of Virginia Woolf's novels.

520   Bodkin, Maud. "The Patterns in Sacred and in Contemporary Literature", ARCHETYPAL PATTERNS IN POETRY: PSYCHOLOGICAL STUDIES OF IMAGINATION, Lond., 1934, 300-307.

About ORLANDO.   "...the tale of ORLANDO is attractive in its rejection of a matter of fact framework for the more imaginative mode of conveying truth".

521   Bowling, Lawrence E. "What is the Stream of Consciousness Technique?" PMLA, 65, 4, June 1950, 339-340.

General remarks on the technique in THE WAVES.

522   Breman, Gerald. SOUTH FROM GRANADA, Lond., 1957, 139-152.

Stresses the close link between Virginia Woolf's work

and the Bloomsbury ethos.

523   Brewster, Dorothy. EAST-WEST PASSAGE: A STUDY IN LITERARY
       RELATIONSHIPS, Lond., 1954, p. 213.

       About the influence of the Russian novelists, particularly
       Dostoevsky, on Virginia Woolf.

524   Brown, E. K. "Interweaving Themes", RHYTHM IN THE NOVEL,
       Toronto, 1950, 64-70.

       Examines the structure of TO THE LIGHTHOUSE. Thinks that
       its three parts are interconnected as the 'three big blocks
       of sound in a sonata'.

525   Bullett, Gerald. MODERN ENGLISH FICTION: A PERSONAL VIEW,
       Lond., 1926, 86-93.

       "Virginia Woolf has created a world; not a world of men and
       women but a world of luminous twilight; queer, vivid, re-
       mote yet real".

526   Carruthers, John. SCHEHERAZADE OR THE FUTURE OF THE ENGLISH
       NOVEL, Lond., 1927, 67-77.

       Praises Mrs. Woolf's sensitive evocation of moods. Re-
       grets the absence from her novels of a solid and firm
       structure.

527   Chapman, Robert T. "Parties ... Parties ... Parties: Some
       Images of the 'Gay Twenties'," ENGLISH, Lond., XXI, No. 111,
       Autumn 1972, 93-97.

       "The social gathering has been a technique used by writers
       as a means of drawing together characters and providing a
       context for a discussion of ideas". Refers to the parties
       in MRS. DALLOWAY and TO THE LIGHTHOUSE.

528   Charques, R. D. CONTEMPORARY LITERATURE AND SOCIAL REV-
       OLUTION, Lond., 1933, pp. 108-114.

       A Marxist attack on Virginia Woolf. Mrs. Woolf is "aloofness
       itself".

529   Church, Richard. BRITISH AUTHORS, Lond., 1943, pp. 87-90.

       An "abnormal appreciation of the passing phenomenon" is

Virginia Woolf's unique contribution to the novel.

530 _____. THE GROWTH OF THE ENGLISH NOVEL, Lond.,
1951, pp. 212-213.

Discusses the importance of Mrs. Woolf's technical experiments.

531 Cohn, Dorritt. "Narrative Monologue; Definition of a
Fictional Style", COMPARATIVE LITERATURE, Eugene, Oregon,
18, Spring 1966, 97-112.

532 Collins, A. S. ENGLISH LITERATURE OF THE 20TH CENTURY,
Lond., 1951, 217-223.

A critical survey of Virginia Woolf's novels. Suggests
that Mrs. Woolf did not deal with the working classes,
because she was not familiar with them. It showed her
"sincerity".

533 Collins, Joseph. THE DOCTOR LOOKS AT LITERATURE, 1923,
pp. 187-190.

Discusses Virginia Woolf's earlier novels from the psychological standpoint.

534 Connolly, Cyril. ENEMIES OF PROMISE, 1938, pp. 62-63.

An indictment of Woolf's technique. Asserts that Mrs.
Woolf's "worst defect" is her "Mandarin style" which tends
to "spin cocoons of language out of nothing".

535 _____. THE CONDEMNED PLAYGROUND AND OTHER ESSAYS,
Lond., 1945, p. 6.

Condemns Mrs. Woolf's method of characterization.

536 Courtney, Janet E. THE WOMEN OF MY TIME, Lond., 1934.

A descriptive account of Virginia Woolf's work.

537 Conwell, Ethel F. THE STILL POINT: THEMES AND VARIATIONS
IN THE WRITINGS OF T. S. ELIOT, COLERIDGE, YEATS, HENRY
JAMES, VIRGINIA WOOLF AND D. H. LAWRENCE, New Brunswick,
New Jersey, 1962.

538 Cross, Wilber L. THE MODERN ENGLISH NOVEL, New Haven,

Connecticut, 1928, pp. 23-25.

Another attack on Mrs. Woolf's character-presentation.

539   Cunliffe, J. W.   ENGLISH LITERATURE IN THE TWENTIETH CEN-
       TURY, New York, 1933, pp. 245-253.

A general consideration of Virginia Woolf's novels up to
THE WAVES.

540   Daiches, David.   THE PRESENT AGE AFTER 1920, Lond., 1958,
       pp. 89-92.

Discusses Virginia Woolf's attempt to render individual
consciousness with the help of her new method.

541   Dataller, Roger (Eaglestone, Archibald).   THE PLAIN MAN
       AND THE NOVEL, Lond., 1940, p. X.

About the common reader's dissatisfaction with Mrs. Woolf's
work.

542   Dobrée, Bonamy.   "The Novel: Had It A Function Today?"
       ESSAYS BY DIVERS HANDS, ed. W. B. Maxwell, Vol. XIII, Lond.,
       1934, pp. 57-76.

Doubts whether Virginia Woolf can at all be called a novelist, because Mrs. Woolf concentrates on the individual consciousness which "weakens" the novel as an art-form.

543   _____.   MODERN PROSE STYLE, Oxford, 1934, 51-54.

544   Drew, Elizabeth.   THE MODERN NOVEL: SOME ASPECTS OF CON-
       TEMPORARY FICTION, New York, 1926, pp. 254-262.

Questions the validity of Mrs. Woolf's method. Comments
on JACOB'S ROOM and MRS. DALLOWAY.

545   Edel, Leon.   "The Novel as Poem", THE PSYCHOLOGICAL NOVEL
       1900-1950, Lond., 1955, pp. 190-202.

A sound examination of the lyricism in Virginia Woolf's
novels.

546   _____.   LITERARY BIOGRAPHY: THE ALEXANDER LEC-
       TURES 1955-1956, Lond., 1957, pp. 89-98.

On ORLANDO. Thinks that the book is not a mere jeu d'
esprit but a "fable" for biographers.

547   Edgar,Pelham. THE ART OF THE NOVEL FROM 1700 TO THE
       PRESENT TIME, New York, 1933, pp. 328-337.

       Calls TO THE LIGHTHOUSE a "masterpiece" for its rare
       combination of "poetry, speculation and character".

548   Eliot, T. S. "Le Roman Anglais Contemporain", LA NOUVELLE
       REVUE FRANCAISE, Paris, May 1927, pp. 669-675.

       Recognizes the importance of Virginia Woolf's innovations
       in the field of fiction. Considers her work "the perfec-
       tion of a type".

549   Ellis, G. U. TWILIGHT ON PARNASSUS: A SURVEY OF POST-
       WAR FICTION AND PRE-WAR CRITICISM, Lond., 1939, pp. 330-
       341.

       Objects to Mrs. Woolf's "preoccupation" with the private
       world.

550   Evans, Ifor B. ENGLISH LITERATURE BETWEEN THE WARS, Lond.,
       1948, pp. 68-74.

       Wonders if the novel as an art form can altogether abandon,
       as Virginia Woolf's novels do, plot, description and action.

551   Fleishman, Avrom. THE ENGLISH HISTORICAL NOVEL: WALTER
       SCOTT TO VIRGINIA WOOLF, Baltimore, Maryland, 1973.

552   Forster, E. M. ASPECTS OF THE NOVEL, 1927, pp. 32-33.

       Finds affinity between Sterne and Mrs. Woolf. Both are
       "fantasists".

553   Fraser, G. S. THE MODERN WRITER AND HIS WORLD, Lond.,
       1964, pp. 115-119.

       Declares that except in TO THE LIGHTHOUSE Mrs. Woolf re-
       mains solitary and detached.

554   Friedman, Melvin. STREAM OF CONSCIOUSNESS: A STUDY IN
       LITERARY METHOD, New Haven, Connecticut, 1955, pp. 178-209.

       Describes Virginia Woolf's use of the stream of consciousness method and the stages of its development from JACOB'S ROOM to THE WAVES.

555   Friedman, Norman. "Criticism and the Novel", THE ANTIOCH REVIEW, Yellow Springs, Ohio, Vol. 18, Fall 1958, pp. 361-365.

Comments on the Clarissa-Septimus relationship in MRS. DALLOWAY. Does not agree with the view that Septimus was Clarissa's "double" and his death could be regarded as "a dynamic self-completion" for her.

556   Friedman, William C. THE ENGLISH NOVEL IN TRANSITION 1885-1940, Norman, Oklahoma, 1942, 214-223.

557   George, W. L. "A Painter's Literature", THE ENGLISH RE-VIEW, Lond., March 1920, pp. 233-234.

Thinks that Virginia Woolf is primarily an impressionist—a painter of the mind. She is detached from the "social impulses and intellectual movements in the masses of mankind". Looks ahead to the anti-aesthetic position on Woolf (See No. 223).

558   Gillett, Eric W. BOOKS AND WRITERS, Singapore, 1930.

559   Gould, Gerald. THE ENGLISH NOVEL OF TO-DAY, Lond., 1924, pp. 183-184.

General comments on JACOB'S ROOM.

560   Grabo, Carl. THE TECHNIQUE OF THE NOVEL, New York, 1928, pp. 297-306.

Disapproves of the structure of JACOB'S ROOM.

561   Greene, Graham. THE LOST CHILDHOOD AND OTHER ESSAYS, Lond., 1951, pp. 69-73.

Complains that Virginia Woolf's characters are little more than "cardboard symbols", because she does not stress the "sense of the importance of the human act".

562   Gregory, Horace. THE SHIELD OF ACHILLES, New York, 1944, pp. 185-193.

Woolf's debt to the 18th century is emphasized. Comments on

Virginia Woolf's interest in the eighteenth century: "The
sensibility which she expressed had its own likeness in the
Age of Sensibility itself".

563 Hampshire, Stuart. MODERN WRITERS AND OTHER ESSAYS, London,
1970.

Psychological approach. Claims that Virginia Woolf "pen-
etrated to levels of experience and of feeling which are
not explored elsewhere".

564 Harwood, H. C. "Recent Tendencies in English Fiction",
THE QUARTERLY REVIEW, Lond., April 1929, p. 323.

Censures Mrs. Woolf's "aloofness" from the world outside
Bloomsbury.

565 Hawkins, E. W. "The Stream of Consciousness Novel", THE
ATLANTIC MONTHLY, Boston, September 1926, pp. 356-360.

Discusses Virginia Woolf's experiments in JACOB'S ROOM
and MRS. DALLOWAY.

566 Heilbrun, C. G. TOWARD A RECOGNITION OF ANDROGYNY, New
York, 1973.

Refers to Virginia Woolf's attack on sexual polarization.

567 Henderson, Philip. THE NOVEL TODAY, Lond., 1936, pp. 23-
28, 87-91 and 246.

A Marxist complaint about Virginia Woolf's withdrawal from
social reality.

568 _____. LITERATURE AND A CHANGING CIVILIZATION,
Lond., 1935, pp. 127-128.

A similar point of view, but less unfavourable.

569 Hoare, D. M. SOME STUDIES IN THE MODERN NOVEL, Lond.,
1938, pp. 36-37.

Discusses Mrs. Woolf's variations on the method of free association.

570 Humphrey, Robert. STREAM OF CONSCIOUSNESS IN THE MODERN
NOVEL, Berkeley, California, 1954, pp. 99-104.

A careful enquiry into Mrs. Woolf's use of symbols in the structural patterns of her four novels: JACOB'S ROOM, MRS. DALLOWAY, TO THE LIGHTHOUSE and THE WAVES.

571   Hyman, Stanley Edgar. "Some Trends in the Novel", COLLEGE ENGLISH, Chicago, 20: October 1958, 1-9.

572   Isaacs, J. AN ASSESSMENT OF TWENTIETH CENTURY LITERATURE, Lond., 1951, pp. 85-88.

Discusses the "musical" pattern of MRS. DALLOWAY and THE WAVES. Traces the influence of R. A. M. Stevenson and Walter Pater on Virginia Woolf's impressionism.

573   Jameson, Storm. "The Georgian Novel and Mr. Robinson", THE BOOKMAN, New York, Vol. LXIX, No. V., July 1929, pp. 449-472.

Maintains that Mrs. Woolf is over-refined and aloof from the "common earth".

574   _____. THE NOVEL IN CONTEMPORARY LIFE, Boston, 1938, pp. 6-7.

Considers THE YEARS a failure.

575   Joad, C. E. M. GUIDE TO MODERN THOUGHT, Lond., 1933, pp. 249-251. Remarks on JACOB'S ROOM. Thinks that its isolated scenes are not interlinked.

576   Johnson, Pamela Hansford. "Literature", THE BALDWIN AGE ed. John Raymond, Lond., 1960, 182-183.

Complains that there is no contact in Virginia Woolf's novels between man and society. THE WAVES is "as remote from the novel of man in society as a novel can be".

577   Johnson, R. B. SOME CONTEMPORARY NOVELISTS (Women), Lond., 1920, pp. 149-160.

A general consideration of the two early novels—THE VOYAGE OUT and NIGHT AND DAY.

578   Kettle, Arnold. AN INTRODUCTION TO THE ENGLISH NOVEL, Lond., Vol. 2, 1953, pp. 100-110.

A left-wing attitude to Virginia Woolf. Criticizes her

"cult of sensibility" which is "inadequately based on the realities of the social situation".

579   Kohler, Dayton. "Time in the Modern Novel", COLLEGE ENG-
       LISH, Illinois, Vol. X, November 1948, pp. 15-20.

       Discusses Virginia Woolf's view of time as duration and
       the conventional concept of time as "a sequence of day and
       night, Monday and Tuesday".

580   Kondo, Ineko. JANE AUSTEN AND VIRGINIA WOOLF, Tokyo, 1956.

581   Kunitz, S. J. and Haycraft,H. TWENTIETH CENTURY AUTHORS,
       New York, 1942, 1548-1550.

582   Lawrence, Margaret. THE SCHOOL OF FEMINITY, New York,
       1937, 373-382.

       Regrets that Virginia Woolf's quiet work "gives hardly
       anything to the modern mind--it is quiet against the row
       of the age".

583   Leavis, F. R. MASS CIVILIZATION AND MINORITY CULTURE,
       Cambridge, 1930, 25-26.

       Associates TO THE LIGHTHOUSE with THE WASTE LAND, ULYSSES
       and HUGH SELWYN MAUBERLEY as "work expressing the finest
       consciousness of the age".

584   _____. THE GREAT TRADITION, Lond., 1948, p. 129.

       Calls Virginia Woolf a mere 'poetizer' who has no profound
       'interest in life'.

585   Leavis, Q. D. FICTION AND THE READING PUBLIC, Lond., 1932,
       222-223 and passim.

       Describes the nature of public reaction to Mrs. Woolf's un-
       conventional novels.

586   Lewis, Wyndham. MEN WITHOUT ART, Lond., 1934, 158-171.

       Attacks Virginia Woolf's subjective technique and alleges
       that MRS. DALLOWAY is "a sort of undergraduate imitation
       of Joyce's ULYSSES".

587   Liddell, Robert. A TREATISE ON THE NOVEL, Lond., 1947,
       92-93.

Criticizes the lack of variety and discrimination in Virginia Woolf's characterization.

588   Logé, Marc. "Quelques Romancieres Anglaises Contemporaines", REVUE POLITIQUE ET LITTERAIRE, Paris, November 21, 1925, 753,756.

589   Lovett, R. M. and Hughes,Helen S. THE HISTORY OF THE NOVEL IN ENGLAND, Boston, 1932, 449-453.

        A descriptive account of Virginia Woolf's novels.

590   MacAfee, Helen. "Some Novelists in Midstream", THE YALE REVIEW, New Haven, January 1926, p. 340.

        Thinks that MRS. DALLOWAY is "akin to an orchestral composition" in its structural perfection.

591   Mackenzie, Compton. LITERATURE IN MY TIME, Lond., 1933, 216-218.

        "Virginia Woolf stands out, not merely as the most vitally creative force among women writers, but as a leader even among men".

592   Magnus, Philip. "A Modern Aspect of the Novel", THE QUARTERLY REVIEW, Lond., January 1936, 61-62.

        Maintains that it is her handling of the time element which constitutes Virginia Woolf's "permanent contribution to the techniques of the novel".

593   Mais, S. P. B. WHY WE SHOULD READ, Lond., 1921, 105-111.

        Describes NIGHT AND DAY as a "penetrating, shrewd comedy wherein many feckless people are portrayed to the life".

594   _____. A CHRONICLE OF ENGLISH LITERATURE, Lond., 1936, p. 331.

        Characterizes MRS. DALLOWAY as an "inverted ULYSSES", because Virginia Woolf "allows the beautiful to override the ugly."

595   Maurois, André. "La Jeune Littérature Anglaise", QUATRE ÉTUDES ANGLAISES, Paris, 1927, Chap. IV, 253-293.

596   McCormic, John. CATASTROPHE AND IMAGINATION, Lond., 1957,
       48-50.

       Discusses the resemblance between Virginia Woolf's exper-
       iments with fiction and those of the Imagists with poetry.

597   Mendilow, A. A. TIME AND THE NOVEL, Lond., 1952, 230 ff.

       A useful discussion of Virginia Woolf's time philosophy.

598   Meyerhoff, Hans. TIME IN LITERATURE, Berkeley, 1955,
       39-40.

       In MRS. DALLOWAY Virginia Woolf "achieves a striking contra-
       puntal effect by interrupting the time flow of the various
       streams of consciousness within the booming of Big Ben".

599   Millett, F. B. CONTEMPORARY BRITISH LITERATURE, Lond.,
       1935, 39-40.

       A general survey of Virginia Woolf's novels.

600   _____. "Feminine Fiction", THE CORNHILL MAGAZINE,
       Lond., Vol. 155, February 1937, 234-235.

601   Mirsky, Dmitri. THE INTELLIGENTSIA OF GREAT BRITAIN,
       translated by Alex Brown, Lond., 1935, 111-120.

       A Marxist attack on Virginia Woolf. Accuses her of ig-
       noring the people outside her 'aristocratic' and 'bourgeois'
       world.

602   Muchnic, Helen. DOSTOEVSKY'S ENGLISH REPUTATION 1881-
       1936 (Smith College Studies in Modern Languages), Northamp-
       ton, Massachusetts, Apr.-June 1939, 144-171.

       On Dostoevsky's influence on Virginia Woolf's conception
       of the novel and her view of time.

603   Muir, Edwin. THE STRUCTURE OF THE NOVEL, Lond., 1928,
       132-133.

       Appreciates the structure of MRS. DALLOWAY.

604   _____. THE PRESENT AGE FROM 1914, Lond., 1939,
       139-140.

       Praises Woolf's power to catch the fleeting impressions,

but dislikes her "baffling remoteness from the root facts of life".

605   Murphy, Dorothy. "Time and the Modern Novel", WATERLOO
       REVIEW 1: Spring 1958, 30-40.

606   Murry, John Middleton. "The Classical Revival", THE ADEL-
       PHI, Lond., 3, 9, February 1926, 585-595.

       Thinks that both JACOB'S ROOM and THE WASTE LAND are
       failures as works of art, because they are "over-intellect-
       ualized /and/ over-laden with calculated subtleties and
       they fail to produce any unity of impression". Murry,
       however, admits that it is not their authors' fault. "They
       wish to express their real experience", but "there is no or-
       der in modern experience".

607   Neill, Diana S. A SHORT HISTORY OF THE ENGLISH NOVEL,
       New York, 1952, 285-293.

       Discusses Mrs. Woolf's poetic sensibility.

608   Nicolson, Nigel. PORTRAIT OF A MARRIAGE, Lond., 1973,
       182-183, 199-206, and passim.
       Victoria Sackville-West wrote to Harold Nicolson about Virginia
       Woolf: "One's love for Virginia is a mental thing, a spiritual
       thing, an intellectual thing, and she inspires a feeling of
       tenderness".

609   Paterson, John. THE NOVEL AS A FAITH; THE GOSPEL ACCORDING
       TO JAMES, HARDY, CONRAD, JOYCE, LAWRENCE AND VIRGINIA WOOLF,
       Gambit, 1973.

610   Peake, Charles. "Defoe and the Modern Novel", BOOKS:
       THE JOURNAL OF THE NATIONAL BOOK-LEAGUE, Lond., May-June
       1960, 79-84.

       About Virginia Woolf's indebtedness to Defoe. She was in-
       fluenced by him in her conception of character and her re-
       jection of the conventional plot in the novel.

611   Phelps, Gilbert. THE RUSSIAN NOVEL IN ENGLISH FICTION, 1966,
       passim.

       Discusses the Woolf-Turgenev relationship. His characteri-
       zation and his sense of form impressed Mrs. Woolf.

612   Pippett, Aileen. "The Birth of Bloomsbury", NEW WORLD

WRITING, New York, Vol. 4, pp. 177-188.

Argues that Virginia Woolf did not "cut herself off from contact with the busy life around her".

613   Priestley, J. B. "Some Reflections of a Popular Novelist", ESSAYS AND STUDIES, published by members of the English Association, Lond., Vol. XVII, 1932, pp. 149-159.

Blames the stream of consciousness as the "sloppiest of all methods in fiction" and maintains that Virginia Woolf is, like Joyce, "a fantastic monologuist" rather than a novelist.

614   Rahv, Philip. IMAGE AND IDEA, Lond., 1957, 167-171.

Complains that the interior monologue of Virginia Woolf, unlike that of Joyce, becomes 'a vehicle of poetic memory' and cuts her characters off from concrete situations in life.

615   Raleigh, John Henry. "Victorian Morals and the Modern Novel", PARTISAN REVIEW, New York, Spring 1958, Vol. XXV, No. 2, pp. 241-264.

Discusses the subjective line in the novel from George Eliot to Virginia Woolf and James Joyce.

616   Rathburn, Robert and Steinmann, Martin, Jr. (eds.). FROM AUSTEN TO JOSEPH CONRAD: ESSAYS COLLECTED IN MEMORY OF JAMES   HILLHOUSE, Minneapolis, 1958, p. 264.

Notices Samuel Butler's influence on Virginia Woolf's aversion to "professionalism" and her "preoccupation with the nature of human identity".

617   Reade, A. R. MAIN CURRENTS IN MODERN LITERATURE, Lond., 1935, pp. 165-178.

A descriptive account of Virginia Woolf's experimental novels up to THE WAVES.

618   Romain, Yvonne de. "L'Evolution du Roman Anglais", REVUE DE POLITIQUE ET DE LITTÉRATURE, Paris, January 3, 1931, 13-20.

619   Routh, H. V. ENGLISH LITERATURE AND IDEAS IN THE TWENTIETH

CENTURY, Lond., 1946, 172-177.

Suggests that "if Joyce's achievement is to be associated with word psychology, Virginia Woolf's is to be associated with clairvoyance".

620   Ruotolo, Lucio P. SIX EXISTENTIAL HEROES: THE POLITICS OF FAITH, Harvard, 1973.

About Clarissa Dalloway.

621   Schorer, Mark. "The Chronicle of Doubt", VIRGINIA QUARTERLY REVIEW, Virginia, XVIII, No. 1, Spring 1942, 200-215. Thinks that Virginia Woolf was a mere impressionist who had no co-ordinated attitude to life. Her work is barren of ideas. "If Virginia Woolf took to writing novels which were more like imagistic poems, that is because she had nothing to say".

622   Scott-James, R. A. FIFTY YEARS OF ENGLISH LITERATURE 1900-1950, Lond., 1951, 142-149.

623   Seward, Barbara. THE SYMBOLIC ROSE, New York, 1960, 127-131.

"Mrs. Woolf used the rose as a minor but recurrent symbol of a highly personel fulfillment ... in her major novels the rose appears in intense moments during which her characters realize the ineffable meanings of their lives".

624   Sitwell, Edith. ENGLISH WOMEN, Lond., 1942, 47-48.

625   Snow, C. P. "Story-Tellers of the Atomic Age", THE NEW YORK TIMES, January 30, 1955, 28-29.

A severe indictment of Virginia Woolf's aestheticism. Snow calls Woolf's work "the most hopeless cul-de-sac in the novel's history", because it has "no roots in society".

626   Spender, Stephen. "The Novel and Narrative Poetry", PEN-GUIN NEW WRITING, Lond., September 1942, 123-132.

Spender maintains that Virginia Woolf's poetic method has actually "resulted in a dilution of the interest in wide aspects of social life".

627   Starkie, Enid. FROM GAUTIER TO ELIOT: THE INFLUENCE OF FRANCE ON ENGLISH LITERATURE 1851-1939, Lond., 1960, 193-197.

About Proust's influence on Virginia Woolf.

628   Steinberg, Erwin. "Freudian Symbolism and Communication",
       LITERATURE AND PSYCHOLOGY, New York, iii, ii, April 1953,
       2-5 and iv, 23-25, 64-65.

       Maintains that the relationship between Clarissa and Peter
       can be interpreted only in tems of Freudian symbols.

629   Stone, Wilfred. THE CAVE AND THE MOUNTAIN: A STUDY OF E.
       M. FORSTER, Stanford, 1966, 371-373.

       Notes the differences between the methods of Virginia Woolf
       and E. M. Forster.

630   Sutton, Denys. DUNCAN GRANT AND HIS WORLD, Lond., 1964
       (Introduction).

       Thinks that Virginia Woolf was not blind to her own age.
       Her novels show "an awareness of contemporary topics".

631   Szladits, Lola L. (ed). OTHER PEOPLE'S MAIL: LETTERS TO
       MEN AND WOMEN OF LETTERS SELECTED FROM THE HENRY W. AND
       ALBERT A. BERG COLLECTION OF ENGLISH AND AMERICAN LITER-
       ATURE, New York Public Library, 1973.

       Contains Virginia Woolf's letter to Barbara Hiles Bagenal.

632   Tindall, William York. THE LITERARY SYMBOL, Bloomington,
       Indiana, 1955, 203-205.

       Comments on the function of the symbols in MRS. DALLOWAY.

633   _____. FORCES IN MODERN BRITISH LITERATURE 1885-
       1956, New York, 1956, 199-205.

       Argues that Woolf's novels are not formless. "In place of
       conventional structure imposed from without, she developed
       flexible organic forms from within". Also discusses
       Bergson's influence on Woolf.

634   Wagenknecht, Edward. CAVALCADE OF THE ENGLISH NOVEL, New
       York, 1943, 522-532.

       A summary of Woolf's novels up to JACOB'S ROOM.

635   Wagner, Geoffrey. "Bloomsbury Revisited", THE COMMONWEAL,

New York, LXV, No. 23, March 8, 1957, 589-590.

A short general discussion of the Bloomsbury Group. Complains that Virginia Woolf and the other Bloomsbury authors were "hopelessly inbred".

636   Ward, A. C. THE NINETEEN-TWENTIES, Lond., 1930, 60-62.

Asserts that Virginia Woolf's work "was not in the direction of anti-realism, but of ultra-realism which consists in the attempt to lay bare the inward experiences and impressions of the characters".

637   Watt, Donald J. "G. E. Moore and the Bloomsbury Group", ENGLISH LITERATURE IN TRANSITION 1880-1920, California, Vol. 12, No. 3, 1969, 119-134.

Discusses the impact of Moore's PRINCIPIA ETHICA on Virginia Woolf and E. M. Forster. Suggests that Virginia Woolf's conception of the autonomy of art was influenced by Moore's philosophy of intrinsic good. Moore believed, as Woolf did, in the intrinsic value of aesthetic enjoyment.

638   Wilson, Angus. "Sense and Sensibility in Recent Writing", THE LISTENER, Lond., August 24, 1950, 279-280.

Declares that Virginia Woolf failed to become a "great novelist because she failed to extend her sympathies outside a narrow class range".

VII. BOOK REVIEWS

A. REVIEWS OF THE NOVELS

    1. THE VOYAGE OUT

        (a) BRITISH NEWSPAPERS:

640   A. N. M. THE MANCHESTER GUARDIAN, April 15, 1915, p. 4.
641   Forster, E. M. THE DAILY NEWS AND LEADER, April 8, 1915, p. 7.
642   Murray, H. THE SUNDAY TIMES, April 4, 1915, p. 5.
643   Unsigned. THE MORNING POST, April 5, 1915, p. 2.
644   _____. THE OBSERVER, April 4, 1915, p. 3.

        (b) BRITISH PERIODICALS:

645   Gould, Gerald. THE NEW STATESMAN, April 10, 1915, pp. 18-19.
646   O'Brien, D. THE TRUTH, April 7, 1915, p. 3.
647   Unsigned. THE ATHENAEUM, May 1, 1915, p. 401.
648   _____. THE BOOKMAN, June 1915, p. 88.
649   _____. COUNTRY LIFE, April 24, 1915, p. 564.
650   _____. THE FIELD, May 15, 1915, p. 855.
651   _____. THE NATION, May 1, 1915, p. 156.
652   _____. THE QUEEN, May 1, 1915, p. 738.
653   _____. THE SATURDAY REVIEW, June 19, 1915, p. iv.
654   _____. THE SPECTATOR, July 10, 1915, pp. 54-55.
655   _____. THE STANDARD, April 9, 1915, p. 3.
656   _____. TIMES LITERARY SUPPLEMENT, April 1, 1915, p. 110.
657   _____. THE WESTMINSTER GAZETTE, April 24, 1915, p. 3.

        (c) AMERICAN NEWSPAPERS:

658   Unsigned. THE NEW YORK TIMES, June 13, 1920, p. 308.

        (d) AMERICAN PERIODICALS:

659   Rourke, Constance Mayfield. THE NEW REPUBLIC, New York, May 5, 1920, pp. 320-322.
660   S. M. R. THE BOOKMAN, New York, June 1920, p. 500.
661   Underhill, Ruth Murray. THE BOOKMAN, New York, August 1920, pp. 685-686.
662   Unsigned. THE INDEPENDENT, New York, July 10, 1920, p. 53.

2. NIGHT AND DAY

(a) BRITISH NEWSPAPERS:

663   Courtney, W. L. THE DAILY TELEGRAPH, November 14, 1919, p. 14.
664   Des, A. THE MANCHESTER GUARDIAN, December 5, 1919, p. 7.
665   Garnett, Edward. THE DAILY NEWS, November 17, 1919, p. 5.
666   Scott-James, R. A. THE DAILY CHRONICLE, October 27, 1919, p. 4.
667   Unsigned. THE GLASGOW HERALD, December 18, 1919, p. 4.
668   _____. THE IRISH TIMES, January 23, 1920, p. 7.
669   _____. THE MORNING POST, November 21, 1919, p. 2.
670   _____. THE SCOTSMAN, December 8, 1919, p. 2.
671   _____. THE WESTMINSTER GAZETTE, December 13, 1919, p. 12.

(b) BRITISH PERIODICALS:

672   A. Wayfarer. THE NATION, November 29, 1919, p. 295.
673   E. A. B. THE NEW COMMONWEALTH, November 21, 1919, p. 5.
674   E. B. C. THE CAMBRIDGE MAGAZINE, November 1, 1919, pp. 49-50.
675   Ellis-Roberts, R. THE BOOKMAN, December 1919, p. 98.
676   George, W. L. THE WORLD, London, December 13, 1919, p. 25.
677   _____. THE ENGLISH REVIEW, March 1920, pp. 233-234.
678   Heseltine, Olive. EVERYMAN, November 6, 1919, p. 114.
679   Howe, P. P. THE FORTNIGHTLY REVIEW, January 1, 1920, pp. 69-.
680   Mansfield, Katherine. THE ATHENAEUM, November 21, 1919, p. 1227.
681   Unsigned. THE ANNUAL REGISTER, 1920, Part II, p. 36.
682   _____. THE FIELD, November 29, 1919, p. 732.
683   _____. THE GRAPHIC, November 29, 1919, p. 778.
684   _____. THE GUARDIAN, December 24, 1919, p. 1357.
685   _____. THE LONDON MERCURY, January 1920, pp. 339-340.
686   _____. THE NATION, May 15, 1920, pp. 228-230.
687   _____. THE OUTLOOK, December 1919, p. 596.
688   _____. TIMES LITERARY SUPPLEMENT, October 30, 1919, p. 607.

(c) AMERICAN NEWSPAPERS:

689   Abbot, Samuel. THE NEW YORK TRIBUNE, October 17, 1920, p. 8.
690   Unsigned. THE NEW YORK TIMES, December 5, 1920, p. 20.

691 _____. THE NEW YORK TRIBUNE, October 17, 1920, p. 8.

692 _____. SPRINGFIELD REPUBLICAN, Massachusetts, December 7, 1920, p. 8.

(d) AMERICAN PERIODICALS:

693 Overton, Grant M. LIFE, November 25, 1920, p. 97.

694 "Simon Pure". THE BOOKMAN, New York, February 1920, p. 547.

695 _____. THE BOOKMAN, New York, March 1920, p. 44.

3. JACOB'S ROOM

(a) BRITISH NEWSPAPERS:

696 A. N. M. THE MANCHESTER GUARDIAN, November 3, 1922, p. 9.

697 Bettany, Lewis. THE DAILY NEWS, October 27, 1922, p. 7.

698 Courtney, W. L. THE DAILY TELEGRAPH, November 10, 1922, p. 4.

699 Turner, W. J. THE DAILY HERALD, November 15, 1922, p. 7.

700 Unsigned. THE DAILY CHRONICLE, November 9, 1922, p. 6.

701 _____. THE IRISH TIMES, November 24, 1922, p. 3.

702 _____. LIVERPOOL DAILY POST AND MERCURY, December 4, 1922, p. 6.

703 _____. THE OBSERVER, November 5, 1922, p. 4.

704 _____. PALL MALL GAZETTE AND GLOBE, October 27, 1922, p. 6.

705 _____. THE WESTMINSTER GAZETTE, November 22, 1922, p. 12.

706 _____. THE YORKSHIRE POST, November 29, 1922, p. 4.

(b) BRITISH PERIODICALS:

707 Gould, Gerald. THE SATURDAY REVIEW, November 11, 1922, p. 726.

708 Harwood, H. C. THE OUTLOOK, November 18, 1922, p. 427.

709 Lynd, Sylvia. TIME AND TIDE, November 24, 1922, pp. 1136-1137.

710 McQuilland, Louis J. JOHN O'LONDON'S WEEKLY, November 11, 1922, p. 221.

711 Milne, James. THE GRAPHIC, December 2, 1922, p. 826.

712 Reid, Forrest. THE NATION AND ATHENAEUM, November 4, 1922, p. 204.

713 Sanders, G. Manning. THE NEW WITNESS, December 22, 1922, p. 397.

714   Shanks, Edward. THE LONDON MERCURY, December 1922,
       p. 210.
715   Sheldon, G. A. THE CAMBRIDGE REVIEW, December 1,
       1922, p. 146.
716   West, Rebecca. THE NEW STATESMAN, November 4, 1922,
       p. 142.
717   Unsigned. THE ANNUAL REGISTER, 1922, Part II, p. 37.
718   _____. THE NEW AGE, December 21, 1922, p. 123.
719   _____. THE QUEEN, December 2, 1922, p. 705.
720   _____. THE SPECTATOR, November 11, 1922, p. 661.
721   _____. TIMES LITERARY SUPPLEMENT, October 26,
       1922, p. 683.

(c) AMERICAN NEWSPAPERS:

722   Broun, Heywood. THE WORLD, New York, March 4, 1923,
       p. 6E.
723   Dark, Sidney. CHICAGO DAILY TRIBUNE, April 7, 1923,
       p. 11.
724   Mavity, Nancy Barr. SAN FRANCISCO CHRONICLE, May 20,
       1923, p. D5.
725   Rascoe, Burton. THE NEW YORK TRIBUNE, February 25,
       1923, p. 17.
726   Unsigned. THE NEW YORK HERALD, February 25, 1925,
       p. 17.
727   _____. THE NEW YORK TIMES, March 4, 1923, p. 11.
728   _____. SAN FRANCISCO CHRONICLE, March 4, 1923,
       p. D5.

(d) AMERICAN PERIODICALS:

729   Bodenheim, Maxwell. THE NATION, March 28, 1923, pp.
       368-369.
730   Bonton, H. W. THE INDEPENDENT, New York, April 14,
       1923, p. 262.
731   Garnett, David. THE DIAL, Chicago, July 1923, pp.
       83-86.
732   MacAfee, Helen. THE BOOKMAN, New York, January 1924,
       p. 514.
733   _____. THE ATLANTIC MONTHLY, Boston, July 1923,
       p. 229.
734   Warwick, Diana. LIFE, New York, February 8, 1925,
       p. 22.
735   Unsigned. THE BOOKMAN, New York, May 1923, p. 326.
736   _____. SPRINGFIELD REPUBLICAN, Massachusetts,
       June 19, 1923, p. 79.

4. MRS. DALLOWAY

(a) BRITISH NEWSPAPERS

737   A. M. A. LIVERPOOL POST AND MERCURY, May 27, 1925,
       p. 4.

738   H. C. O'N. THE WESTMINSTER GAZETTE, June 10, 1925,
      p. 6.
739   Royde-Smith, N. G. THE DAILY NEWS, May 28, 1925,
      p. 4.
740   T. M. THE MANCHESTER GUARDIAN, June 5, 1925, p. 7.
741   Unsigned. THE BIRMINGHAM POST, June 5, 1925, p. 3.
742   _____. THE GLASGOW HERALD, June 1, 1925, p. 7.
743   _____. THE IRISH TIMES, June 5, 1925, p. 3.
744   _____. THE MORNING POST, May 19, 1925, p. 9.
745   _____. THE OBSERVER, May 24, 1925, p. 4.
746   _____. THE SCOTSMAN, May 14, 1925, p. 2.

(b) BRITISH PERIODICALS:

747   Bullett, Gerald. THE SATURDAY REVIEW, May 30, 1925,
      p. 588.
748   Harwood, H. C. THE OUTLOOK, May 23, 1925, p. 346.
749   _____. THE SPECTATOR, June 27, 1925, pp. 1050-
      1051.
750   Holms, J. F. THE CALENDAR OF MODERN LETTERS, July
      1925, pp. 404-405.
751   Kennedy, P. C. THE NEW STATESMAN, June 6, 1925, p.
      229.
752   Languish, Lydia. JOHN O'LONDON'S WEEKLY, June 13,
      1925, p. 340.
753   Lynd, Sylvia. TIME AND TIDE, May 15, 1925, p. 472.
754   Unsigned. THE ADELPHI, August 1925, p. 230.
755   _____. THE ANNUAL REGISTER, 1925, Part II, pp.
      50-51.
756   _____. COUNTRY LIFE, June 6, 1925, p. 916.
757   _____. THE ENGLISH REVIEW, July 1925, p. 147.
758   _____. TIMES LITERARY SUPPLEMENT, May 21, 1925,
      p. 349.

(c) AMERICAN NEWSPAPERS:

759   Crawford, John W. THE NEW YORK TIMES, May 10, 1925,
      p. 10.
760   _____. THE WORLD, New York, May 10, 1925, p. 4M.
761   J. W. C. THE WORLD, New York, June 7, 1925, p. 4M.
762   Parsons, Alice Beal. THE NEW YORK HERALD TRIBUNE,
      May 31, 1925, p. 5.
763   Unsigned. THE CHRISTIAN SCIENCE MONITOR, Boston,
      June 3, 1925, p. 8.

(d) AMERICAN PERIODICALS:

764   D. R. THE INDEPENDENT, New York, June 20, 1925, p.
      703.
765   Hughes, Richard. THE SATURDAY REVIEW OF LITERATURE,
      New York, May 16, 1925, p. 755.
766   J. F. THE BOOKMAN, New York, July 1925, p. 586.

96

767 Krutch, Joseph Wood. THE NATION, New York, June 3, 1925, pp. 631-632.
768 MacAfee, Helen. THE YALE REVIEW, New Haven, January 1926, p. 340.
769 Unsigned. THE DIAL, Chicago, October 1925, p. 352.
770 _____. LIFE, New York, July 2, 1925, p. 27.

5. TO THE LIGHTHOUSE

   (a) BRITISH NEWSPAPERS:

   771 A. M. THE MANCHESTER GUARDIAN, May 20, 1927, p. 9.
   772 A. M. A. LIVERPOOL POST AND MERCURY, May 11, 1927, p. 4.
   773 Bennett, Arnold. THE EVENING STANDARD, June 23, 1927, p. 5.
   774 Brown, Francis. THE DAILY HERALD, May 23, 1927, p. 7.
   775 Gould, Gerald. THE DAILY NEWS, May 16, 1927, p. 4.
   776 _____. THE OBSERVER, May 15, 1927, p. 8.
   777 Unsigned. THE BIRMINGHAM POST, May 20, 1927, p. 3.
   778 _____. THE DAILY TELEGRAPH, May 27, 1927, p. 17.
   779 _____. THE GLASGOW HERALD, May 26, 1927, p. 4.
   780 _____. THE IRISH TIMES, May 27, 1927, p. 5.
   781 _____. THE MORNING POST, June 21, 1927, p. 5.

   (b) BRITISH PERIODICALS:

   782 Annand, Rachel. THE SPECTATOR, May 14, 1927, p. 871.
   783 Heseltine, Olive. TIME AND TIDE, June 17, 1972, p. 573.
   784 Languish, Lydia. JOHN O'LONDON'S WEEKLY, June 11, 1927, p. 283.
   785 Muir, Edwin. THE NATION AND ATHENAEUM, July 2, 1927, p. 450.
   786 Robinson, M. THE NEW ADELPHI, Vol. 1, No. 1, September 1927, pp. 82-83.
   787 Royde-Smith, Naomi. THE NEW STATESMAN, June 4, 1927, pp. 251-252.
   788 Shanks, Edward. THE LONDON MERCURY, July 1927, pp. 323-324.
   789 Sydenham, John. THE EMPIRE REVIEW, July 1927, pp. 73-74.
   790 V. H. F. COUNTRY LIFE, May 21, 1927, p. 816.
   791 Welbey, T. Earle. THE SATURDAY REVIEW, May 7, 1927, pp. 712-713.
   792 Williams, Orlo. THE CRITERION, July 1927, p. 28.
   793 Unsigned. THE BOOKMAN, July 1927, pp. 242-243.
   794 _____. THE ENGLISH REVIEW, July 1927, pp. 114-115.
   795 _____. THE NEW AGE, September 8, 1927, p. 227.
   796 _____. PUNCH, July 27, 1927, p. 84.

797   Unsigned. TIMES LITERARY SUPPLEMENT, May 5, 1927,
        p. 315.

(c) AMERICAN NEWSPAPERS:

798   Clark, Edwin. THE NEW YORK TIMES, June 26, 1927,
        p. 23.
799   Colum, Mary M. THE NEW YORK HERALD TRIBUNE, May 8,
        1927, Section 7, pp. 1 and 6.
800   Kronenberger, Louis. THE NEW YORK TIMES, May 8,
        1927, p. 2.
801   Suckow, Ruth. THE WORLD, New York, May 22, 1927,
        p. 8M.
802   Unsigned. SAN FRANCISCO CHRONICLE, May 22, 1927, p.
        10.

(d) AMERICAN PERIODICALS:

803   Aiken, Conrad. THE DIAL, Chicago, July 1927, pp. 41-
        44.
804   C. S. and M. A. THE WOMAN CITIZEN, New York, June
        1927, p. 37.
805   Cuttung, Elizabeth Brown. THE NORTH AMERICAN REVIEW,
        New York, June-July-August 1927, pp. 331-332.
806   F. W. K. THE SEWANEE REVIEW, July 1927, pp. 365-366.
807   Gale, Zona. THE SATURDAY REVIEW OF LITERATURE, New
        York, June 25, 1927, pp. 928-929.
808   Humphray, Mary Churchill. THE VIRGINIA QUARTERLY RE-
        VIEW, Vol. 4, 1928, pp. 128-129.
809   P. L. THE NEW REPUBLIC, New York, June 1, 1927, pp.
        50-51.
810   Ross, Mary. THE NATION, New York, July 20, 1927, pp.
        67-68.
811   Walker, Charles R. THE INDEPENDENT, New York, May
        28, 1927, p. 567.
812   Unsigned. THE BOOKMAN, New York, July 1927, p. 521.
813   _____. TIME, New York, May 30, 1927, pp. 39-40.

6. ORLANDO

(a) BRITISH NEWSPAPERS

814   A. M. A. LIVERPOOL POST AND MERCURY, October 17,
        1928, p. 4.
815   Bennett, Arnold. THE EVENING STANDARD, November 8,
        1928, p. 7.
816   H. I. A. F. THE MANCHESTER GUARDIAN, November 12,
        1928, p. 5.
817   MacCarthy, Desmond. THE SUNDAY TIMES, October 14,
        1928, p. 10.
818   S. P. B. M. THE DAILY TELEGRAPH, October 19, 1928,
        p. 16.
819   Squire, J. C. THE OBSERVER, October 21, 1928, p. 6.

820 Unsigned. THE BIRMINGHAM POST, October 30, 1928, p. 4.
821 _____. THE DAILY MAIL, October 11, 1928, p. 21.
822 _____. THE GLASGOW HERALD, October 25, 1928, p. 4.
823 _____. THE IRISH TIMES, November 2, 1928, p. 3.
824 _____. THE YORKSHIRE POST, October 24, 1928, p. 4.

(b) BRITISH PERIODICALS:

825 Friedlaender, V. H. COUNTRY LIFE, October 27, 1928, pp. 576-577.
826 Gates, Barrington. THE NATION AND ATHENAEUM, October 27, 1928, pp. 148-150.
827 Harwood, H. C. THE QUARTERLY REVIEW, April 29, 1929, pp. 323-324.
828 Joyce, Michael. THE NEW AGE, January 31, 1929, p. 165.
829 Rees, Richard. THE NEW ADELPHI, December 1928, p. 185.
830 Smith, Clara. TIME AND TIDE, October 12, 1928, p. 943.
831 Turnell, G. M. THE CAMBRIDGE REVIEW, November 2, 1928, p. 100.
832 Unsigned. THE ENGLISH REVIEW, December 1928, p. 734.
833 _____. LIFE AND LETTERS, Vol. 1, No. 6, 1928, pp. 514-516.
834 _____. THE NEW STATESMAN, November 10, 1928, pp. 162-164.
835 _____. PUNCH, October 24, 1928, p. 474.
836 _____. THE SATURDAY REVIEW, October 13, 1928, p. 474.
837 _____. THE SPECTATOR, October 20, 1928, p. 547.
838 _____. TIMES LITERARY SUPPLEMENT, October 11, 1928, p. 729.

(c) AMERICAN NEWSPAPERS:

839 Butcher, Fanny. CHICAGO DAILY TRIBUNE, December 15, 1928, pp. 13-15.
840 Chase, Cleveland B. THE NEW YORK TIMES, October 21, 1928, p. 7.
841 Crattan, C. Hartley. THE WORLD, New York, November 11, 1928, p. 10M.
842 Pritchett, V. S. THE CHRISTIAN SCIENCE MONITOR, Boston, November 14, 1928, p. 11.
843 Swinnerton, Frank. CHICAGO DAILY TRIBUNE, December 1, 1928, p. 24.
844 West, Rebecca. THE NEW YORK HERALD TRIBUNE, October 21, 1928, Section XI, pp. 1 and 6.
845 Unsigned. SAN FRANCISCO CHRONICLE, October 21, 1928, p. 10D.

(d) AMERICAN PERIODICALS:

846   Aiken, Conrad. THE DIAL, Chicago, February 1929, pp.
       147-149.
847   Brewster, Dorothy. THE NATION, New York, November
       28, 1928, pp. 577-578.
848   Brickell, Herschel. THE NORTH AMERICAN REVIEW, Bos-
       ton, Vol. 226, December 1928, Adv.
849   Canby, Henry Seidel. THE SATURDAY REVIEW OF LITER-
       ATURE, New York, November 3, 1928, p. 313.
850   Githens, Perry. LIFE, New York, November 30, 1928,
       p. 24.
851   Lawrence, S. Morris. THE BOOKMAN, New York, December
       1928, pp. 460-461.
852   MacAfee, Helen. THE YALE REVIEW, New Haven, Vol. 18,
       1929, p. XVI.
853   Myers, Walter L. THE VIRGINIA QUARTERLY REVIEW, Vir-
       ginia, Vol. V, 1929, pp. 299-306.
854   Robbins, Francis Lamont. OUTLOOK AND INDEPENDENT,
       New York, November 21, 1928, p. 1210.
855   Troy, William. THE NEW REPUBLIC, New York, November
       21, 1928, pp. 23-24.
856   Unsigned. THE PUBLISHER'S WEEKLY, New York, October
       27, 1928, p. 1745.
857   _____. TIME, New York, October 22, 1928, p. 45.

7. THE WAVES

(a) BRITISH NEWSPAPERS:

858   A. M. A. LIVERPOOL POST AND MERCURY, October 14,
       1931, p. 4.
859   C. M. THE MANCHESTER GUARDIAN, October 23, 1931,
       p. 5.
860   Gould, Gerald. THE OBSERVER, October 11, 1931, p. 8.
861   Herbert, Alice. THE YORKSHIRE POST, October 14, 1931,
       p. 6.
862   Lynd, Sylvia. NEWS CHRONICLE, October 14, 1931, p.
       4.
863   Pippett, Roger. THE DAILY HERALD, October 8, 1931,
       p. 18.
864   Shackleton, Edith. THE EVENING STANDARD, October 8,
       1931, p. 18.
865   Swinnerton, Frank. THE EVENING NEWS, October 9, 1931,
       p. 18.
866   V. A. C. THE MORNING POST, October 13, 1931, p. 4.
867   West, Rebecca. THE DAILY TELEGRAPH, October 16, 1931,
       p. 16.
868   Unsigned. THE BIRMINGHAM POST, October 20, 1931, p.
       4.
869   _____. THE DAILY MIRROR, October 12, 1931, p. 21.
870   _____. THE GLASGOW HERALD, October 15, 1931, p. 4.
871   _____. THE SCOTSMAN, December 3, 1931, p. 2.

872   Unsigned. THE SUNDAY TIMES, November 29, 1931, p. 9.

873   _____. THE TIMES, October 9, 1931, p. 6.

(b) BRITISH PERIODICALS:

874   Arrowsmith, J. E. S. THE LONDON MERCURY, December 1931, pp. 204-205.

875   Bullett, Gerald. THE NEW STATESMAN AND NATION, October 10, 1931, p. X.

876   Hartley, L. P. THE WEEK-END REVIEW, October 24, 1931, p. 518.

877   Harwood, H. C. THE SATURDAY REVIEW, October 10, 1931, p. 462.

878   Holtby, Winifred. TIME AND TIDE, October 10, 1931, pp. 1163-1164.

879   _____. THE BOOKMAN, December 1931, p. 184.

880   Jameson, Storm. THE FORTNIGHTLY REVIEW, November 1931, pp. 677-678.

881   Jones, E. B. C. THE ADELPHI, December 1931, pp. 188-189.

882   Kendon, Frank. JOHN O'LONDON'S WEEKLY, October 24, 1931, p. 124.

883   Nicolson, Harold. ACTION, October 8, 1931, p. 8.

884   Renny, Peter. THE EMPIRE REVIEW, December 1931, p. 417.

885   Scott, Mcnair. THE ENGLISH REVIEW, November 1931, p. 753.

886   Strong, L. A. C. THE SPECTATOR, October 10, 1931, p. 470.

887   Williams, Orlo. THE NATIONAL REVIEW, December 1931, pp. 829-830.

888   Unsigned. COUNTRY LIFE, October 31, 1931, p. 491.

889   _____. THE GUARDIAN, October 30, 1931, p. 751.

890   _____. PUNCH, October 21, 1931, p. 446.

891   _____. THE QUARTERLY REVIEW, April 1932, p. 216.

892   _____. THE REVIEW OF REVIEWS, October 15, 1931, p. 10.

893   _____. TIMES LITERARY SUPPLEMENT, October 8, 1931, p. 773.

(c) AMERICAN NEWSPAPERS:

894   Butcher, Fanny. CHICAGO DAILY TRIBUNE, December 12, 1931, p. 21.

895   Kronenberger, Louis. THE NEW YORK TIMES, October 25, 1931, p. 5.

896   Pritchett, V. S. THE CHRISTIAN SCIENCE MONITOR, Boston, November 21, 1931, p. 10.

897   West, Rebecca. THE NEW YORK HERALD TRIBUNE, November 1, 1931, pp. 1 and 6.

898   Unsigned. THE NEW YORK HERALD TRIBUNE, November 15, 1931, p. 27.

899   Unsigned. SAN FRANCISCO CHRONICLE, December 6,
        1931, p. 2B

(d)   AMERICAN PERIODICALS:

900   Brickell, Herschell. THE NORTH AMERICAN REVIEW,
        New York, December 1931, p. 573.
901   Daniels, Earl. THE SATURDAY REVIEW OF LITERATURE,
        New York, December 5, 1931, p. 352.
902   Hartley, Lodwick C. THE SOUTH ATLANTIC QUARTERLY,
        July 1932, pp. 349-351.
903   MacAfee, Helen. THE YALE REVIEW, Winter 1931, p.
        vi.
904   Myers, Walter L. THE VIRGINIA QUARTERLY REVIEW,
        Vol. 8, 1932, pp. 110-111.
905   Rose, Virgilia Peterson. THE OUTLOOK AND INDEPENDENT,
        New York, November 11, 1931, p. 344.
906   Sykes, Gerald. THE NATION, New York, December 16,
        1931, pp. 674-675.
907   Unsigned. THE BOOKMAN, New York,December 1931, pp.
        383-385.
908   _____. THE FORUM, New York, February 1932, p.
        XIV.
909   _____. THE PUBLISHERS' WEEKLY, New York, December
        5, 1931, p. 2493.
910   _____. TIME, Chicago, October 19, 1931, pp. 63-
        64.

8.   THE YEARS

(a)   BRITISH NEWSPAPERS:

911   A. M. H. LIVERPOOL DAILY POST, March 17, 1937, p. 7.
912   Bates, H. E. THE MORNING POST, March 30, 1937, p. 6.
913   Brophy, John. THE DAILY TELEGRAPH, March 16, 1937,
        p. 6.
914   Gibson, Wilfred. THE MANCHESTER GUARDIAN, March 16,
        1937, p. 7.
915   Hale, Lionel. NEWS CHRONICLE, March 17, 1937, p. 6.
916   MacCarthy, Desmond. THE SUNDAY TIMES, May 9, 1937,
        p. 8.
917   Pippett, Roger. THE DAILY HERALD, March 18, 1937,
        p. 8.
918   Selincourt, Basil D. THE OBSERVER, March 14, 1937,
        p. 5.
919   Unsigned. THE EVENING STANDARD, March 18, 1937, p.
        10.
920   _____. THE BIRMINGHAM POST, March 16, 1937, p. 4.
921   _____. THE GLASGOW HERALD, May 18, 1937, p. 4.
922   _____. THE SCOTSMAN, March 18, 1937, p. 17.
923   _____. THE TIMES, March 19, 1937, p. 10.

(b) BRITISH PERIODICALS:

924 Bennett, Joan. THE CAMBRIDGE REVIEW, June 9, 1937, p. 496.
925 Bosanquet, Theodora. TIME AND TIDE, March 13, 1937, pp. 352-353.
926 Church, Richard. JOHN O'LONDON'S WEEKLY, March 19, 1937, pp. 1019-1021.
927 Garnett, David. THE NEW STATESMAN, March 20, 1937, p. 481.
928 Johnson, Pamela Hansford. THE ENGLISH REVIEW, April 1937, p. 508.
929 Mellers, W. H. SCRUTINY, June 1937, pp. 71-75.
930 Muir, Edwin. THE LISTENER, March 31, 1937, p. 622.
931 Olivier, Edith. COUNTRY LIFE, April 3, 1937, pp. 358-359.
932 Scott-James, R. A. THE LONDON MERCURY, April 1937, 629-631.
933 Spalding, M. LIFE AND LETTERS TODAY, Summer 1937, p. 156.
934 Sparrow, John. THE SPECTATOR, March 19, 1937, p. 526.
935 Williams, Orlo. THE CRITERION, July 1937, pp. 714-716.
936 Unsigned. PUNCH, March 17, 1937, p. 307.
937 _____. THE SATURDAY REVIEW, March 20, 1937, p. 200.
938 _____. TIMES LITERARY SUPPLEMENT, March 13, 1937, p. 185.

(c) AMERICAN NEWSPAPERS:

939 Butcher, Fanny. CHICAGO DAILY TRIBUNE, April 10, 1937, p. 8.
940 Jack, Peter M. THE NEW YORK TIMES, April 11, 1937, Section 7, p. 1.
941 Paterson, Isabel. THE NEW YORK HERALD TRIBUNE, April 11, 1937, Section X, pp. 1 and 2.
942 Pritchett, V. S. THE CHRISTIAN SCIENCE MONITOR, Boston, March 31, 1937, p. 10.
943 Unsigned. SAN FRANCISCO CHRONICLE, May 9, 1937, p. D5.

(d) AMERICAN PERIODICALS:

944 Eshleman, Lloyd W. THE COMMONWEAL, New York, July 23, 1937, p. 329.
945 Hicks, Granville. THE NEW REPUBLIC, New York, April 28, 1937, p. 363.
946 MacAfee, Helen. THE YALE REVIEW, Vol. 26, 1937, p. X.
947 Roberts, John Hawley. THE VIRGINIA QUARTERLY REVIEW, Vol. 13, 1937, pp. 437-439.
948 Stevens, George. THE SATURDAY REVIEW OF LITERATURE, New York, April 10, 1937, p. 5.

949 Troy, William. THE NATION, New York, April 24,
     1937, pp. 473-474.
950 Unsigned. NEWSWEEK, New York, April 10, 1937, p.
     32.
951 _____. THE PUBLISHERS' WEEKLY, New York, April
     10, 1937, p. 1615.
952 _____. TIME, New York, April 12, 1937, pp. 93-
     96.
953 _____. THE WILSON BULLETIN FOR LIBRARIANS, New
     York, November 1937, p. 168.

9. BETWEEN THE ACTS

  (a) BRITISH NEWSPAPERS:

     954 Bishop, George W. THE DAILY TELEGRAPH, July 18,
          1941, p. 3.
     955 Brighouse, Harold. THE MANCHESTER GUARDIAN, July
          25, 1941, p. 3.
     956 Lynd, Robert. NEWS CHRONICLE, July 31, 1941, p. 2.
     957 MacCarthy, Desmond. THE SUNDAY TIMES, July 20,
          1941, p. 3.
     958 Swinnerton, Frank. THE OBSERVER, July 20, 1941, p.
          5.
     959 Unsigned. THE BIRMINGHAM POST, July 22, 1941, p. 2.
     960 _____. THE GLASGOW HERALD, July 19, 1941, p. 3.
     961 _____. THE SCOTSMAN, July 17, 1941, p. 7.

  (b) BRITISH PERIODICALS:

     962 Bates, H. E. THE FORTNIGHTLY REVIEW, September 1941,
          p. 312.
     963 Bosanquet, Theodore. TIME AND TIDE, July 19, 1941,
          pp. 605-606.
     964 Bowen, Elizabeth. THE NEW STATESMAN AND NATION, July
          19, 1941, pp. 63-64.
     965 Bryher,   . LIFE AND LETTERS TO-DAY, September
          1941, pp. 195-197.
     966 Cecil, David. THE SPECTATOR, July 18, 1941, p. 64.
     967 Church, Richard. JOHN O'LONDON'S WEEKLY, August 29,
          1941, p. 353.
     968 Hartley, L. P. SKETCH, August 13, 1941, p. 118.
     969 Leavis, F. R. SCRUTINY, January 1942, pp. 295-298.
     970 Lehmann, John. NEW WRITING AND DAYLIGHT, Summer
          1942, p. 158.
     971 Muir, Edwin. THE LISTENER, July 24, 1941, p. 139.
     972 Widdows, Margharita. THE ANNUAL REGISTER, 1941,
          Part II, p. 322.

  (c) AMERICAN NEWSPAPERS:

     973 Ross, Mary. THE NEW YORK HERALD TRIBUNE, October 5,
          1941, p. 7.

974   Strode, Hudson. THE NEW YORK TIMES, October 5,
       1941, Section 6, p. 1.
975   Stull, Christopher. SAN FRANCISCO CHRONICLE,
       October 12, 1941, p. 13.
976   Thompson, Ralph. THE NEW YORK TIMES, October 2,
       1941, p. 23.

(d) AMERICAN PERIODICALS:

977   Adey, Alvin. CURRENT HISTORY, New York, November
       1941, p. 275.
978   Cowley, Malcolm. THE NEW REPUBLIC, New York, October
       6, 1941, p. 440.
979   Jones, Howard M. THE SATURDAY REVIEW OF LITERATURE,
       October 25, 1941, p. 7.
980   Kronenberger, Louis. THE NATION, New York, October
       11, 1941, pp. 344-345.
981   Rosenberg, Harold. THE PARTISAN REVIEW, New York,
       Vol. 9, No. 1, January-February 1942, pp. 87-88.
982   Taylor, Helene Scheroff. THE LIBRARY JOURNAL, New
       York, October 1, 1941, p. 841.
983   Unsigned. NEWSWEEK, New York, October 13, 1941, p.
       78.
984   _____. TIME, New York, October 13, 1941, pp. 103-
       104.

3. REVIEWS OF NON-FICTION

1. MONDAY AND TUESDAY (1921)

985   Eliot, T. S. THE DIAL, New York, August 1921, 216-
       217.
986   E. S. THE LONDON MERCURY, July 1921, p. 321.
987   West, Rebecca. THE YALE REVIEW, July 1923, 849-850.
988   Anonymous. THE TIMES LITERARY SUPPLEMENT, Lond.,
       April 7, 1921, p. 227.

2. KEW GARDENS (1919)

989   Anonymous. THE CRITERION, Lond., January 1928, p.
       87.
990   _____. THE TIMES LITERARY SUPPLEMENT, Lond.,
       May 29, 1919, p. 293.

3. MR. BENNETT AND MRS. BROWN (1924)

991   Ellis-Williams, A. THE SPECTATOR, Lond., January
       10, 1925, p. 47.
992   Morris, Feiron. THE CRITERION, Lond., Vol. III, No.
       10, January 1925, 326-329.

4. THE COMMON READER (1925)

993　Collins, H. P.　THE CRITERION, Lond., July 1925,
586-588.
994　E. R.　THE CALENDAR　OF MODERN LETTERS, Lond., Vol.
1, No. 4, June 1925, 320-322.
995　Anonymous.　THE TIMES LITERARY SUPPLEMENT, Lond.,
May 7, 1925, p. 313.

5. A ROOM OF ONE'S OWN (1929)

996　Bosanquet, Theodore.　TIME AND TIDE, Lond., November
15, 1929, 1371-1372.
997　Squire, J. C.　THE OBSERVER, Lond., December 22,
1929, p. 4.
998　West, Rebecca.　THE BOOKMAN, New York, January 1930,
553-554.
999　Williams, Orlo.　THE CRITERION, Lond., Vol. IX,
April 1930, 509-512.
1000　Woodbridge, Elizabeth.　THE YALE REVIEW, New Haven,
Vol. 19, Spring 1930, 627-629.
1001　Anonymous.　THE ENGLISH REVIEW, Lond., December 1929,
782-783.
1002　_____.　THE GLASGOW HERALD, October 31, 1929, p.
4.
1003　_____.　THE NEW YORK TIMES, January 14, 1931, p.
22.
1004　_____.　THE SATURDAY REVIEW, Lond., November 23,
1929, p. 615.
1005　_____.　THE TIMES LITERARY SUPPLEMENT, Lond.,
October 31, 1929, p. 867.

6. THE COMMON READER:　SECOND SERIES (1932)

1006　Chew, S. C.　THE YALE REVIEW, December 1932, p. 390.
1007　French, Yvonne.　THE LONDON MERCURY, December 1932,
p. 173.
1008　Gorman, W. J.　THE NEW REPUBLIC, New York, February
8, 1933, p. 357.
1009　Manson, Aelfric.　THE DUBLIN REVIEW, July 1933, 135-
137.
1010　P. H.　THE NEW YORK TIMES, November 13, 1932, p. 2.
1011　Powell, Dilys.　THE SUNDAY TIMES, October 16, 1932,
p. 12.
1012　Renny, Peter.　THE EMPIRE REVIEW, Lond., November
1932, p. 303.
1013　Sackville-West, Victoria.　THE WEEK-END REVIEW,
Lond., October 1933, p. 352.
1014　Selincourt, Basil de.　THE OBSERVER, Lond., October
23, 1932, p. 8.
1015　Sparrow, John.　THE SPECTATOR, Lond., November 4,
1932, p. 636.

1016	Spender, Stephen. THE CRITERION, Lond., April 1933, 522-524.
1017	Thomson, Denys. SCRUTINY, Lond., December 1932, 288-289.
1018	Anonymous. THE NEW YORK TIMES, November 13, 1932, p. 2.
1019	_____. PUNCH, Lond., October 26, 1932, p. 474.
1020	_____. THE SATURDAY REVIEW, Lond., October 22, 1932, p. 428.
1021	_____. THE TIMES, Lond., October 28, 1932, p. 17.

7. FLUSH (1933)

1022	Chilton, E. C. THE ENGLISH REVIEW, Lond., November 1933, p. 557.
1023	Farquhar, Jean. THE LONDON MERCURY, December 1933, p. 174.
1024	Gordon, W. R. NEWS CHRONICLE, Lond., October 11, 1933, p. 7.
1025	MacCarthy, Desmond. THE SUNDAY TIMES, Lond., October 8, 1933, p. 6.
1026	Macaulay, Rose. THE SPECTATOR, Lond., October 6, 1933, 450-451.
1027	Sackville-West, Victoria. THE WEEK-END REVIEW, Lond., October 1933, p. 352.
1028	Scovell, E. J. TIME AND TIDE, Lond., October 14, 1932, p. 1234.
1029	Smith, S. M. THE NINETEENTH CENTURY, Lond., December 1933, p. XXIII.
1030	Anonymous. THE GLASGOW HERALD, October 5, 1933, p. 4.
1031	_____. LIFE AND LETTERS, Lond., December 1933, February 1934, 494-496.
1032	_____. THE TIMES LITERARY SUPPLEMENT, Lond., October 5, 1933, p. 667.

8. THREE GUINEAS (1938)

1033	Allen, Agnes. THE SATURDAY REVIEW OF LITERATURE, New York, August 27, 1938, p. 6.
1034	Bosanquet, Theodore. TIME AND TIDE, Lond., June 4, 1938, 788-790.
1035	Chase, Mary Ellen. THE YALE REVIEW, Vol. 38, 1939, 403-405.
1036	Colum, Mary M. THE FORUM, New York, November 1938, p. 226.
1037	E. H. W. QUEEN'S QUARTERLY, Kingston, Ontario, Autumn 1938, p. 418.
1038	Greene, Graham. THE SPECTATOR, Lond., June 17, 1938, 1110-1112.
1039	John, K. THE NEW STATESMAN AND NATION, June 11, 1938, 995-996.

1040   Leavis, Q. D. SCRUTINY, Lond., Vol. VII, No. 2,
        September 1938, 203-214.
1041   Lynd, Robert. NEWS CHRONICLE, Lond., June 3, 1938,
        p. 4.
1042   Pippett, Roger. THE DAILY HERALD, June 2, 1938,
        p. 14.
1043   Selincourt, Basil de. THE OBSERVER, June 5, 1938,
        p. 5.
1044   Stocks, Mary. THE MANCHESTER GUARDIAN, June 10,
        1938, p. 7.
1045   Woods, Katherine. THE NEW YORK TIMES, August 28,
        1938, p. 5.
1046   Young, G. M. THE SUNDAY TIMES, June 19, 1938, p. 7.
1047   Anonymous. THE SATURDAY REVIEW, Lond., June 11,
        1938, p. 374.
1048   _____. THE TIMES, Lond., June 3, 1938, p. 20.
1049   _____. THE TIMES LITERARY SUPPLEMENT, Lond.,
        June 4, 1938, p. 379.

9. ROGER FRY (1940)

1050   B. M. THE DALHOUSIE REVIEW, Halifax, Nova Scotia,
        Vol. XXI, No. 3, October 1941, p. 379.
1051   Bentley, E. C. THE DAILY TELEGRAPH, August 3, 1940,
        p. 3.
1052   Finlayson, Donald L. THE YALE REVIEW, Vol. 30, No.
        2, December 1940, 395-398.
1053   Lynd, Robert. NEWS CHRONICLE, Lond., July 24, 1940,
        p. 4.
1054   MacCarthy, Desmond. THE SUNDAY TIMES, Lond., Aug-
        ust 4, 1940, p. 4.
1055   Maccoll, D. S. THE OBSERVER, August 4, 1940, p. 2.
1056   Newton, Eric. THE MANCHESTER GUARDIAN, August 13,
        1940, p. 7.
1057   Porteus, Hugh Gordon. TIME AND TIDE, August 17,
        1940, p. 848.
1058   Read, Herbert. THE SPECTATOR, Lond., August 2,
        1940, p. 124.
1059   Waley, Arthur. THE LISTENER, Lond., August 15, 1940,
        p. 243.
1060   Anonymous. THE TIMES, Lond., July 27, 1940, p. 9.
1061   _____. THE TIMES LITERARY SUPPLEMENT, July 27,
        1940, p. 364.

10. THE DEATH OF THE MOTH AND OTHER ESSAYS (1942)

1062   Anand, Mulk Raj. LIFE AND LETTERS, Lond., October
        1942, 56-58.
1063   Bishop, George. THE DAILY TELEGRAPH, Lond., June
        12, 1942, p. 3.
1064   Colum, Mary M. THE NEW YORK HERALD TRIBUNE, October
        4, 1942, p. 3.

1065   Dent, Alan. JOHN O'LONDON'S WEEKLY, Lond., July 3, 1942, p. 127.
1066   H. K. PUNCH, Lond., June 10, 1942, p. 492.
1067   Kronenberger, Louis. THE NATION, New York, October 17, 1942, 382-385.
1068   MacCarthy, Desmond. THE SUNDAY TIMES, Lond., June 14, 1942, p. 3.
1069   Rahv, Philip. KENYON REVIEW, Ohio, Vol. 5, 1943, 147-151.
1070   Schorer, Mark. THE YALE REVIEW, December 1942, 377-381.
1071   Stewart, Carol. THE SPECTATOR, Lond., June 19, 1942, 585-586.
1072   Tindal, Martin. TIME AND TIDE, Lond., June 20, 1942, 506-507.
1073   Anonymous. NOTES AND QUERIES, Lond., January 30, 1943, p. 89.
1074   _____. TIMES LITERARY SUPPLEMENT, Lond., June 13, 1942, p. 296.

11. A HAUNTED HOUSE AND OTHER SHORT STORIES (1944)

1075   Bennett, Joan. THE NEW STATESMAN, February 26, 1944, p. 144.
1076   Brace, Marjorie. ACCENT ANTHOLOGY, New York, 1946, 246-251.
1077   Brighouse, Harold. THE MANCHESTER GUARDIAN, February 1944, p. 3.
1078   Godwin, W. H. THE CAMBRIDGE REVIEW, May 13, 1944, p. 325.
1079   Kavan, Anna. HORIZON, Lond., April 1944, p. 284.
1080   Lynd, Robert. NEWS CHRONICLE, Lond., February 16, 1944, p. 2.
1081   MacCarthy, Desmond. THE SUNDAY TIMES, Lond., February 6, 1944, p. 3.
1082   Muir, Edwin. THE LISTENER, Lond., March 2, 1944, p. 250.
1083   O'Brien, Kate. THE SPECTATOR, Lond., March 3, 1944, p. 204.
1084   Smith, Steve. JOHN O'LONDON'S WEEKLY, February 5, 1944, 13-14.
1085   Tindal, Martin. TIME AND TIDE, Lond., March 4, 1944, p. 202.
1086   Young, Marguerite. KENYON REVIEW, Ohio, Vol. 7, 1945, 149-151.
1087   Anonymous. TIME, Chicago, April 24, 1944, p. 34.
1088   _____. THE TIMES LITERARY SUPPLEMENT, Lond., February 12, 1944, p. 77.

12. THE MOMENT AND OTHER ESSAYS (1948)

1089   A. R. JOHN O'LONDON'S WEEKLY, Lond., January 9, 1948, p. 2.

1090   Bennett, Joan. THE CAMBRIDGE REVIEW, May 1, 1948,
        45-47.
1091   Bradenham, Hugh. LIFE AND LETTERS, Lond., May
        1948, 171-173.
1092   Connolly, Cyril. THE NEW YORKER, April 10, 1948,
        101-105.
1093   MacCarthy, Desmond. THE SUNDAY TIMES, Lond., Decem-
        ber 2, 1947, p. 3.
1094   Nicolson, Harold. THE DAILY TELEGRAPH, Lond., Jan-
        uary 2, 1948, p. 3.
1095   Pacey, David. THE UNIVERSITY OF TORONTO QUARTERLY,
        Vol. 17, April 1948, p. 241.
1096   Paterson, Isabel. NEW YORK HERALD TRIBUNE, March
        28, 1948, p. 3.
1097   Pritchett, V. S. THE NEW STATESMAN, December 27,
        1948, p. 511.
1098   Savage, D. S. THE SPECTATOR, Lond., December 19,
        1947, p. 778.
1099   Tindal, Martin. TIME AND TIDE, Lond., January 3,
        1948, p. 15.
1100   Trilling, Diana. THE NEW YORK TIMES, March 21,
        1948, p. 1.
1101   Woodbridge, Homer E. THE YALE REVIEW, Vol. 37, No.
        4, June 1948, p. 732.
1102   Anonymous. TIME, Chicago, April 5, 1948, p. 48
1103   _____. THE TIMES LITERARY SUPPLEMENT, February
        7, 1948, p. 80.

13. THE CAPTAIN'S DEATH BED AND OTHER ESSAYS (1950)

1104   A. R. JOHN O'LONDON'S WEEKLY, May 26, 1950, p. 306.
1105   Betjamin, John. THE DAILY HERALD, Lond., May 17,
        1950, p. 6.
1106   Bogan, Louise. THE NEW REPUBLIC, New York, May 29,
        1950, 18-19.
1107   Bolton, Isabel. NEW YORK HERALD TRIBUNE, June 11,
        1950, p. 4.
1108   Gillett, Eric. THE NATIONAL AND ENGLISH REVIEW,
        Lond., August 1950, p. 223.
1109   Hopkins, Gerard. TIME AND TIDE, Lond., May 27,
        1950, p. 535.
1110   Muggeridge, Malcolm. THE DAILY TELEGRAPH, Lond.,
        May 12, 1950, p. 6.
1111   Nicolson, Harold. THE OBSERVER, Lond., May 11,
        1950, p. 7.
1112   Pritchett, V. S. THE NEW STATESMAN AND NATION,
        May 13, 1950, p. 548.
1113   Redman, Ben Ray. THE SATURDAY REVIEW OF LITERATURE,
        New York, June 17, 1950, p. 17.
1114   Anonymous. THE TIMES LITERARY SUPPLEMENT, Lond.,
        May 19, 1950, p. 319.

14. A WRITER'S DIARY (1953)

1115   Auden, W. H. THE NEW YORKER, March 6, 1954, 99-
       104.
1116   Bowen, Elizabeth. THE NEW YORK TIMES, February 21,
       1954, pp. 1 and 6.
1117   Daiches, David. THE TWENTIETH CENTURY, Lond.,
       December 1953, 482-485.
1118   _____. THE MANCHESTER GUARDIAN, November 10,
       1953, p. 4.
1119   Doner, Dean. THE WESTERN REVIEW, Iowa, Vol. 18,
       Summer 1954, p. 324.
1120   Geismar, Maxwell. THE NATION, New York, February
       27, 1954, 176-176.
1121   Gillett, Eric. THE NATIONAL REVIEW, Lond., Decem-
       ber 1953, 372-373.
1122   Godden, Rumer. NEW YORK HERALD TRIBUNE, February
       21, 1954, p. 1.
1123   Green, Henry. THE LONDON MAGAZINE, February 1954,
       80-83.
1124   Hafley, James. ACCENT, Illinois, Spring 1954, 156-
       159.
1125   Hughes, Richard. THE SPECTATOR, Lond., November 20,
       1953, 587-588.
1126   J. R. THE DAILY TELEGRAPH, Lond., November 13,
       1953, p. 8.
1127   Jackson, David. MUSEUM NOTES, Rhode Island School
       of Design, Providence, Rhode Island, U.S.A., Vol.
       12, No. 1, Fall 1954, 9-12.
1128   Lewin, Ronald. JOHN O'LONDON'S WEEKLY, November 13,
       1953, p. 5.
1129   Mortimer, Raymond. THE SUNDAY TIMES, Lond., Novem-
       ber 1, 1953, p. 5.
1130   Nicolson, Benedict. THE NEW STATESMAN AND NATION,
       November 7, 1953, 567-568.
1131   Plomer, William. THE TIMES LITERARY SUPPLEMENT,
       Lond., August 6, 1954, p. ii.
1132   Poore, Charles. THE NEW YORK TIMES, February 18,
       1954, p. 29.
1133   Powell, Anthony. PUNCH, Lond., November 18, 1953,
       p. 614.
1134   Quennell, Peter. THE DAILY MAIL, Lond., November
       13, 1953, p. 6.
1135   Schorer, Mark. THE NEW REPUBLIC, New York, March 1,
       1954, 18-19.
1136   Spring, Howard. COUNTRY LIFE, Lond., November 26,
       1953, 1759.
1137   Weeks, Edward. THE ATLANTIC MONTHLY, Boston, April
       1954, p. 80.
1138   Wilson, Angus. THE OBSERVER, Lond., November 1,
       1953, p. 9.
1139   Anonymous. THE GLASGOW HERALD, November 12, 1953,
       p. 3.
1140   _____. THE TIMES, Lond., November 4, 1953, p.
       10.

1141   Anonymous. THE TIMES LITERARY SUPPLEMENT, Lond.,
        November 20, 1953, p. 742.

15. VIRGINIA WOOLF AND LYTTON STRACHEY: LETTERS,edited by
    Leonard Woolf and James Strachey (1956)

    1142   Allen, Walter. THE NATION, New York, January 26,
            1957, 81-82.
    1143   Moore, Harry T. THE NEW YORK TIMES, December 30,
            1956, p. 14.
    1144   Mortimer, Raymond. THE SUNDAY TIMES, Lond., Novem-
            ber 18, 1956, p. 4.
    1145   Muggeridge, Malcolm. THE NEW REPUBLIC, New York,
            January 28, 1957, 16-17.
    1146   Nicolson, Harold. THE OBSERVER, Lond., November 18,
            1956, p. 10
    1147   Poore, Charles. THE NEW YORK TIMES, December 19,
            1956, p. 13.
    1148   Pritchett, V. S. THE NEW STATESMAN AND NATION,
            November 17, 1956, 641-642.
    1149   Anonymous. THE TIMES, Lond., November 15, 1956, p.
            13.
    1150   _____. THE TIMES LITERARY SUPPLEMENT, Lond.,
            December 7, 1956, p. 721.

16. GRANITE AND RAINBOW: ESSAYS (1958)

    1151   Bennett, Joan. THE CAMBRIDGE REVIEW, October 18,
            1958, 45-47.
    1152   Corke, Hilary. ENCOUNTER, Lond., August 1958, 87-
            88.
    1153   Cosman, Max. THE COMMONWEAL, New York, November
            1958, 155-156.
    1154   Garnett, David. TIME AND TIDE, Lond., July 5, 1958,
            p. 828.
    1155   Lerman, Leo. THE AMERICAN SCHOLAR, Virginia, U.S.A.,
            Vol. 2, Winter 1958-59, p. 246.
    1156   Welty, Eudora. THE NEW YORK TIMES, September 21,
            1958, p. 6.
    1157   Anonymous. THE LONDON MAGAZINE, Vol. 5, No. 10,
            October 1958, pp. 60-62.
    1158   _____. THE TIMES, Lond., June 19, 1958, p. 13.
    1159   _____. THE TIMES LITERARY SUPPLEMENT, July 4,
            1958, p. 369.

17. CONTEMPORARY WRITERS, edited by Jean Guiguet (1965)

    1160   Plomer, William. THE LISTENER, Lond., December 2,
            1965, p. 911.
    1161   Seymour-Smith, Martin. THE SPECTATOR, Lond., Novem-
            ber 26, 1965, 698-699.

1162   Watson, George. THE REVIEW OF ENGLISH STUDIES,
        Lond., Vol. xviii, No. 69, February 1967, 96-97.
1163   Anonymous. THE NEW YORKER, September 17, 1966.

18 COLLECTED ESSAYS, edited by Leonard Woolf, Vols. 1 and 2
    (1966)

    1164   Anderson, Patrick. THE SPECTATOR, Lond., November
            11, 1966, 620-621.
    1165   Brooke, Jocelyn. THE LISTENER, Lond., October 27,
            1966, 621-622.
    1166   Pritchett, V. S. THE NEW STATESMAN, Lond., Novem-
            ber 25, 1966, p. 790.
    1167   Anonymous. THE TIMES, Lond., October 20, 1966, p.
            16.

19 COLLECTED ESSAYS, edited by Leonard Woolf, Vols. 3 and 4
    (1967)

    1168   Anderson, Patrick. THE SPECTATOR, Lond., September
            8, 1967, p. 273.
    1169   Hall, Donald. THE NEW YORK TIMES, December 24, 1967,
            p. 1.
    1170   Laski, Margharita. THE LISTENER, Lond., October 26,
            1967, pp. 543-544.

BIBLIOGRAPHIES

1   Beebe, Maurice. "Criticism of Virginia Woolf: A Selected
      Checklist with an Index to Studies of Separate Works,"
      MODERN FICTION STUDIES, Lafayette, II, i, February 1956,
      36-45.

2   Corney, C. P. Section on Virginia Woolf in THE NEW CAM-
      BRIDGE BIBLIOGRAPHY OF ENGLISH LITERATURE, Cambridge Uni-
      versity Press, 1972, Vol. 4.

3   Novak, Jane. "Recent Criticism of Virginia Woolf: Janu-
      ary 1970-June 1972: Abstracts of Published Criticism and
      Unpublished Dissertations."

      VIRGINIA WOOLF QUARTERLY, San Diego, California, 1: i,
      1972, 141-155.

4   Torien, B. J. A BIBLIOGRAPHY OF VIRGINIA WOOLF, 1882-
      1941, Cape Town, 1943.

5   Weiser, Barbara. "Criticism of Virgina Woolf from 1956 to
      the Present: A Selected Checklist with an Index to Studies
      of Separate Works", MODERN FICTION STUDIES, Lafayette, 18:
      Autumn 1972, 477-486.

      A supplement to the checklist by Maurice Beebe which ap-
      peared in MODERN FICTION STUDIES in Spring 1956. Divided
      into general studies of Woolf's individual works of fic-
      tion. Unpublished dissertations, book reviews, and mater-
      ial in foreign languages are excluded.

****

I. CRITICS AND REVIEWERS